ELMHURST PUBLIC LIBRARY

3 1135 00987 5623

W9-AMB-097

The Roots of Things

811.54
Kumin, M.

THE ROOTS OF THINGS

— ESSAYS —

MAXINE KUMIN

ELMHURST PUBLIC LIBRARY
125 S. PROSPECT AVE.
ELMHURST, IL 60126

NORTHWESTERN UNIVERSITY PRESS

EVANSTON, ILLINOIS

Northwestern University Press
www.nupress.northwestern.edu

Copyright © 2010 by Maxine Kumin. Published 2010 by Northwestern
University Press. All rights reserved.

Printed in the United States of America

10 9 8 7 6 5 4 3 2 1

Library of Congress Cataloging-in-Publication Data

Kumin, Maxine, 1925–
    The roots of things : essays / Maxine Kumin.
        p. cm.
    Collected essays, some previously published or delivered as speeches.
    Includes bibliographical references.
    ISBN 978-0-8101-2648-0 (pbk. : alk. paper) 1. Kumin, Maxine, 1925–
2. American poetry—20th century—History and criticism. I. Title.
PS3521.U638R66 2010
811.54—dc22

                                                      2009037821

♾ The paper used in this publication meets the minimum requirements of the
American National Standard for Information Sciences—Permanence of Paper
for Printed Library Materials, ANSI Z39.48-1992.

Most of what is happening is hidden.
There is a subworld
Where the roots of things exist.

—MAY SWENSON

CONTENTS

ACKNOWLEDGMENTS

Many of the essays in this book have been published elsewhere or were delivered as speeches.

I. Taking Root

"Growing Up on British Books" was originally published as "E. Nesbit and Primrose Cumming" in *Twice-Told Children's Tales: The Influence of Childhood Reading on Writers for Adults,* ed. Betty Greenway (New York: Routledge, 2005).

"Swift to Its Close" was published in *Shenandoah* 59, no. 1 (Spring/Summer 2009).

"The Horses of Childhood" was published in *Equestrian Magazine* circa 1967.

II. Poets and Poetry

"The Revision of Emily D." was published as "Emily Revisited" in *The Emily Dickinson Journal* 15, no. 2 (Fall 2006). Copyright © 2006 The Johns Hopkins University Press. Reprinted with permission of The Johns Hopkins University Press.

"On Receiving the Frost Medal," a speech, was shown from a DVD at the Poetry Society of America's annual awards ceremony, May 12, 2006.

The brief speech at the Poetry Society of America's laureates' dinner was delivered October 12, 2005.

"Celebrating Josephine Jacobsen, 1997 Frost Medal Winner" was a speech to the Poetry Society of America, delivered April 25, 1997.

The introduction to *Carolyn Kizer: Perspectives on Her Life and Work,* ed. Annie Finch, Johanna Keller, and Candace McClelland (Fort Lee, N.J.: CavanKerry Press, 2001), is reprinted with permission.

"Cats in Zanzibar" was published in *The Writer's Chronicle* 35, no. 6 (Summer 2003).

"Audience" was published in *The Eye of the Poet: Six Views of the Art and Craft of Poetry,* ed. David Citino (New York: Oxford University Press, 2001).

"Letter to a Young Writer" was published in *Teachers & Writers* 33, no. 4 (March/April 2002). Reprinted with permission.

"Notes on 'Pantoum, with Swan'": the poem was first published in *The Literary Review* 44, no. 1 (Fall 2000).

"The Poet on the Poem: Contexts and Connections" was published in *The American Poetry Review* 35, no. 5 (September/October 2006).

"Taking a Stand: If This Be Treason, Make the Most of It" first appeared in *Planet on the Table: Poets on the Reading Life,* ed. Sharon Bryan and William Olsen (Louisville, Ky.: Sarabande Books, 2003).

The entry in *Poet's Bookshelf* was included in *Poet's Bookshelf: Contemporary Poets on Books That Shaped Their Art,* ed. Peter Davis (Selma, Ind.: Barnwood Press, 2005).

"On 'Four Poems About Jamaica,' by William Matthews" was published in *Poetry International* 9 (2005). The poems are reprinted with permission of the William Matthews estate.

"On Jane Kenyon" was published as "Dinner at Jane and Don's" in *Simply Lasting: Writers on Jane Kenyon,* ed. Joyce Peseroff (St. Paul, Minn.: Graywolf Press, 2007). It is reprinted with permission of Graywolf Press.

"Longfellow's Antislavery Poems" was a speech delivered at the Maine Historical Society's Centennial Symposium in Portland, November 10, 2007.

The introduction to *Perched on Nothing's Branch: Selected Poems,* by Attila Jószef (Buffalo, N.Y.: White Pine Press, 1999), is reprinted with permission of White Pine Press.

The foreword to *Vive o muere,* by Anne Sexton, translated by Julio Más Alcaraz (Madrid: Vitruvio Press, 2008), is reprinted with permission of Julio Más Alcaraz.

The foreword to *The Complete Love Poems of May Swenson,* by May Swenson (Boston: Houghton Mifflin, 2003), is copyright © 2003 by Maxine Kumin. It is reprinted by permission of Houghton Mifflin Harcourt Publishing Company. All rights reserved.

III. Country Living

"Geese-Go-South Moon" was published in *Yankee Magazine's Seasons* (August 2003).

The foreword to *Say This of Horses: A Selection of Poems,* ed. C. E. Greer and Jenny Kander (Iowa City: University of Iowa Press, 2007), is reprinted by permission of University of Iowa Press.

"Beautiful Soup" was published in *Accent on Lifestyle* (February/March 2006).

"The Wings of Winter" was published in *OnEarth* 27, no. 4 (Winter 2006).

"High Ground" first appeared in the January/February 2003 issue of *Horticulture Magazine.* It is reprinted with permission from *Horticulture* (www.hortmag.com).

"Bear" was published in *Accent* (July/August 2003). It was adapted from an article published in *Country Journal.*

"How We Found Our Dog" was published in *Bark Magazine,* November/December 2008. It is reprinted with permission.

"Settled In at Home" first appeared in *New Hampshire Home* (Spring/ Summer 2007).

THE ROOTS OF THINGS

I. TAKING ROOT

The Singer Sewing Machine

In the thirties, I attended Charles W. Henry Elementary School in Germantown, then a sleepy suburb of Philadelphia. School was a sturdy down-one-hill-and-up-the-other one-mile walk from our house, and I trudged there and back twice a day. In those days, kids walked home for lunch and returned for afternoon classes, which consisted of home economics for the girls and shop for the boys. No one questioned this arrangement. It was simply a given. In sixth grade we girls went to sewing class, presided over in real life and half a hundred nightmares by a supreme harridan named Miss Morrison.

At the front of the room an oilcloth chart the size of a pull-down map of South America displayed the steps to be followed in threading this diabolical invention, the Singer sewing machine. This is my garbled recollection of the eight steps, as foreign to me as a Sanskrit text. First you set the spool on a little spindle, then you gingerly coaxed the thread end through one little eyelet, then you drew this spidery thread across the top to another eyelet, then down and around a small cog. Next you looped the thread under an upside-down hook, then crossed to another eyelet, finally down to the foot, after which you trepidatiously threaded the needle and lowered it with an abrupt snap—think spider trapping its prey—to catch the bobbin thread. That's if you were lucky and had wound the bobbin correctly. (Winding the bobbin was another exercise in arcana.) Once these two threads had mated, you placed your right hand on the flywheel drawing it authoritatively toward you and at the same instant began to pump the treadle, one foot slightly behind the other. At this point the thread invariably broke, flew out of its several eyelets, and you began again.

I could swim the Australian crawl, post to the trot, and smack a softball past third base, but I could not coordinate the flywheel and the treadle. My thread, so painstakingly arranged, broke and flew out of its settings. The bobbin thread, so assiduously wound, drawn up from its little coffin and conjoined with the needle, snapped free and retreated underground. Prisoner of clumsiness, I was told to begin again. "Follow the chart at the front of the room," Miss Morrison said grimly.

Eventually matters got personal. Why couldn't I follow directions? Was there something the matter with my eyesight? Why did my fingers tremble? She disliked my hair, in two long fat braids that I was to scissor off the next year, to my mother's dismay. I was terrified of Miss Morrison, who hinted that my hair was dirty, that it harbored disease, and that if I didn't master the Singer, I would receive an F in her class and be forced to repeat home economics another year. O Sisyphus! *Follow the chart at the front of the room.* I sat frozen at the prospect, then put my head down and to my great surprise threw up all over the machine. A horrified Miss Morrison sent me to the nurse, who called my mother, who rescued me. Miraculously, I was excused from home economics the rest of the term and allowed to spend that period in the school's little library, rereading my old favorites.

To this day I like to think of Miss Morrison, imprisoned by my vomit, cleaning her perfect Singer eyelet by eyelet, visited by the gods' own vengeance.

GROWING UP ON BRITISH BOOKS

The fourth child and only girl in a family of football enthusiasts, I grew up a voracious reader, hiding out in the nooks and crannies of an old Victorian house and, at the appropriate season, under the sheltering limbs of an ancient copper beech. Two books I literally wore out with rereadings have remained as vivid for me today in my eighty-first year as they were when I was eleven and twelve. I even remember how they came to me. Christmas of 1936, after I had adamantly insisted I wanted no present other than a book, I received a collection of E. Nesbit books: *The Story of the Treasure Seekers, The Wouldbegoods,* and *The New Treasure Seekers,* which I have conflated into one enormous tome threatening, even when new, to burst its bindings. My mother was furious when, a few days later, I complained that I had nothing to read. She couldn't believe I had finished it already, so she leafed through and quizzed me about characters and events. After I had convinced her, she demanded that I read it over again, word by word, and stalked away.

Edith Nesbit Bland (1858–1924), a British fabulist who hid behind her first initial, invented six motherless siblings in an Edwardian household of somewhat straitened circumstances. The next-to-oldest, Oswald, tells the story of the Bastables in the third person, inviting readers to guess which Bastable he is (it didn't take long). Dora, the oldest, is the most sensible and least imaginative. H. O.—this always reminded me of H. O. Oats, a hot cereal I detested—is the youngest. Sometimes he "blubbers"

7

and wants to go home. Nesbit's children live an unsupervised life quite separate from the adults. Busy trying to restore the fallen fortunes of the family, they move from one scrape to another, often employing inverted logic toward noble causes. In one episode they misunderstand the phrase "long lost, my grandmother!" and undertake a heroic search for this charming young woman. The Bastables really "would be good" if they could, much as we all would when we were children.

The Bastable children—Dora, Oswald, Dicky, Alice, Noel, and H. O.—long not for ponies but for a perfect household free of financial worries, a mother, and an endless childhood full of adventures. But after the first dire imitation-jungle episode in *The Wouldbegoods* has them banished to the country (an ideal venue for further adventures), they solemnly sign a manifesto of sorts that urges them to be good and to keep a journal toward that end. Through several volumes the endearing Bastables struggle and, luckily for the reader, fail to reach that goal.

On June 6, 1937, for my twelfth birthday I was given *Silver Snaffles,* a magical story by another British author, Primrose Cumming, who was only twenty-three when she wrote it. Tattles, a pony, responds to Jenny's fervent wish to learn how to ride by whispering from his stall, "Through the Dark Corner and the password is Silver Snaffles." Jenny obeys and finds herself in a sunlit world where articulate ponies with good English-country-squire manners and highly individual personalities give lessons in equitation and stable management to some eager, horseless youngsters. After several instructive episodes, the story culminates in a joyous hunt staged by the foxes themselves (here, a shadow of doubt crept in but I brushed it away), who are also great conversationalists. Jenny, launched as a rider, learns that she is to be given a pony of her own. Now she must relinquish her right to the magic password and to the dark corner of Tattles's stall through which she has melted every evening into a better world. I thought it the saddest ending in the entire history of literature.

Eventually, I wore this book out with ritual rereadings; somehow it disappeared from my life. When, forty-odd years later, I assumed my duties at the Library of Congress as poet laureate, it occurred to me that *Silver Snaffles* was undoubtedly housed in that huge repository. The day I found it in the cavernous stacks I carried it up to the Poetry Room that overlooks the Capitol and the Mall and read the story all over again, savoring the parts I had remembered verbatim. While affairs of state were being conducted only a few hundred yards away, I patted the sturdy blue cover and wept.

I think I was crying for my lost childhood, but I'm still not sure. The profound cathartic effect of the book was not assuaged for me by Jenny's acquiring a pony of her own. Nothing would compensate for that loss of innocence, the unworldliness that had enabled her to speak the password and walk into a kingdom of virtue and honor. There, all the ponies were Platonic philosopher-kings, and the children, their willing pupils, rose with pure hearts through the ranks of Becoming to the heightened state of Being represented by well-mucked stalls, well-ridden and chatty equines, and steaming bran mashes.

It was good to grow up on these and other British books: Lewis Carroll's *Alice,* Robert Louis Stevenson's *A Child's Garden of Verses* and, later, *Treasure Island,* and George Fyler Townsend's translations of *Aesop's Fables.* I had of course read the Bobbsey Twins and Nancy Drew books, and even skimmed through my brothers' Tom Swifts, but the writing in all of these was leaden. E. Nesbit and Primrose Cumming at just the right time in my life presented a rich contrast. Their language was lively, unexpected, even lyrical in places. And I fell in love with British spelling, clinging to *favour* and *colour* and *savour* on into high school. I argued with the teacher when these were marked misspellings, and I still *favour* these usages even though I can no longer go "through the Dark Corner" into a better world.

Swift to Its Close

"Swift to its close ebbs out life's little day." That line opens the second verse of "Abide with Me," the hymn my mother played on the organ in the Methodist church of Radford, Virginia. The year was 1912. My mother was sixteen. The church choir rose and dutifully sang all eight verses, written by Henry Lyte in 1847 just three weeks before he died of tuberculosis, and later set to music by William Henry Monk.

I swam miles to the first two verses, humming the words underwater, when I was a member of the Radcliffe College swimming team in the 1940s in Cambridge, Massachusetts. Because I wasn't a sprinter—I couldn't get off the block quickly enough—I mastered distances instead. The 400-meter freestyle was my best event. To stay fit for it I grueled forty minutes or so through chlorinated water every day except Sunday, when the pool was closed.

"SWIFT . . . to its CLOSE . . . ebbs OUT . . . life's LIT . . . tle DAY," I bubbled, smacking the water extra hard wth my left hand on *out* as I tilted my head to the right, just high enough to get a bite of air. Humming underwater isn't as bizarre as it sounds; lots of competitive swimmers do it. It helps to relieve the tedium of a workout. But what was that redundant *out* doing there? I imagined consumptive Henry Lyte, whose breath was ebbing, seizing on it to fill his pentameter line. As I somersaulted, flipped, and pushed off into the turns, I tried out substitutions: "thus EBBS our little day, now EBBS, ebbs NOW, runs OUT, leaks DOWN." I liked the last one best because its assonance picked up the *k-l-s* sounds of *close*. I also liked thinking of this hymn being played religiously before the kickoff of all Rugby Challenge Cup finals. So British, so sportive.

But this story is about my mother, Bella (Doll) Simon, number six in a family of twelve children born to an Orthodox Jewish couple, the only Jews in the little town of Radford in 1896. I have no proof of their Orthodoxy except the size of their family. My grandfather was obeying the biblical command to be fruitful and multiply; my mother could barely remember a year when her mother wasn't pregnant. But they didn't keep a kosher house or go to temple. The nearest one was forty miles away in Roanoke, accessible on the Norfolk & Western. For the High Holidays my grandfather escorted the entire family to this distant synagogue that accommodated his and other outlying clans on Rosh Hashanah and Yom Kippur. Beyond that, their religious expression was limited to the blessing my grandfather said on Friday nights as his wife lit the candles.

My mother had been taking piano lessons for several years, and while no one else in the family was particularly musical, she was said to show considerable aptitude. When Reverend Powell, the Methodist church minister and a good customer in A. Simon & Sons General Store, told my grandfather that his church was mourning the sudden death of their organist, my mother was promptly promoted. I can imagine her there in her shirtwaist and long skirt, hightop shoes, her curly hair, which was ever her despair, pulled back into a sort of chignon. The late afternoon sun sent colored shafts of light through the stained-glass windows where saints unknown to my mother looked benignly on the scene below. At first the organ was daunting. The pedals were new; the sounds she created under her fingers were ocean-deep and alarming. So much power!

My mother took her responsibilities as organist very seriously. Most days she went directly from school to church to rehearse hymns the reverend had selected to be sung the next Sunday: "Just as I Am, Without One Plea," "Day Is Dying in the West," or "A Mighty Fortress Is Our God." Sometimes her sister Polly, only eleven months younger, went with her, just to listen and daydream as the velvety chords rose to mingle with the dyed sun motes streaming in through the upper part of the nave. Sometimes strangers slipped in, just to listen. The church was never locked.

I don't think my grandfather ever opened a church hymnal. Had he read "Hold Thou Thy cross before my closing eyes," the first line of the eighth stanza of "Abide with Me," he might have thought better of lending his middle child to the Methodists. And it wasn't just on Sunday mornings. There were weddings and funerals. "Abide with Me" got quite a workout at funerals.

The next year, Polly ran off with a drummer. My grandfather shut the store down and set out in hot pursuit. By the time the guilty couple was found—in Birmingham, Alabama—Polly, just sixteen, was pregnant. Hearing this cautionary tale from my mother when I turned sixteen, I thought Polly had run away with a real musician. I didn't know *drummer* was a term for traveling salesman.

Where had Polly met this nice-looking, sweet-talking man? In church, as my mother practiced "All Things Bright and Beautiful" one day and "Amazing Grace" the next. Two weeks of spooning in the back pew and she was gone, spirited away on the Norfolk & Western by the drummer from Topeka, Kansas. My mother, torn between propriety and loyalty to Polly, had helped her pack. She had crept out of the third-floor room they shared and tiptoed ahead of her, down the two flights, testing the treads for creaks as she went. Together they slipped through the kitchen, soothing the family black Lab, who slept on a mat next to the stove, with bits of a dinner roll Polly had hidden in her pocket. My mother cautiously undid the heavy lock to the back door and watched as Polly eased out onto the stoop, then, still on tiptoe, scurried out to the road. A dark shape materialized there and the two forms melted into one.

Of course, I am filling in these romantic details. In fact, I am making them up out of whole cloth, as the saying goes, because my mother never described how Polly ran away. But the germ of truth remains: she never told. Never told all those years ago, under relentless questioning. Never told until the day she told me.

"There was no baby," my mother said when I asked. "It was taken care of," she said, in the same passive verbal construction as today's "mistakes were made." I was old enough to guess that Polly had had an abortion. By the time I knew her, she had found a kindly Jewish husband, a lower-echelon lawyer in Philadelphia, and survived a vicious attack of encephalitis, which had left her with gross tremors. They had no children, which, according to my mother, was a blessing. Eleven siblings, my mother included, had settled in the City of Brotherly Love. The twelfth, my Uncle Saul, had joined the army, trained mules for the cavalry in World War I, and spent the rest of his long life in his hometown serving as unofficial ombudsman for the returning servicemen of his and several subsequent wars.

But how could a pious, or only semi-pious, Jewish father arrange an abortion for his daughter, his pretty Paulina? After her twelve pregnancies, I could understand his wife's willingness to expunge her daughter's mistake. Still, if my mother knew about Polly, others in the family must have known, too. In a small town, wouldn't there have been talk? And abortions were notoriously dangerous. Wouldn't it have been better to have Polly stay in Birmingham until the baby was born, then put it up for adoption?

Her father shook her like a kitten in a dog's jaws. He made her jump rope until she dropped. He beat her till she bled. He forced her to swallow a whole glass of castor oil. He sat her in an icy bath for hours. These were the rumors that swirled through Radford. None of them sound like the decent shopkeeper on Main Street whose name was carved in stone over the doorway.

This was the year my mother won the elocution prize, the year she played "Clair de Lune" in a piano recital at the town hall. Was her heart heavy for Polly? Not necessarily, for my mother had once confessed to me shreds of their sibling rivalry. A budding seamstress as an eight-year-old, my mother painstakingly fashioned dresses for her dolls. Polly would snatch these away, substituting her own, whose outfits consisted of a ragged piece of cloth in which holes had been torn for the head and arms. "Oh, let her have them," her mother would scold, "she's younger than you." Younger and out of the way, I reasoned. My mother must have felt some relief.

Soon after Polly was returned to the family, my mother was sent to Philadelphia to live with one of her married older sisters. Her unspoken mission was to find a husband, but suitable men were in short supply. World War I had absorbed many. She commuted by trolley to the Coombs Conservatory of Music and settled down to study the classical repertory, piano harmony, and technique, and began to participate in ensemble programs. Her progress was steady if unremarkable. Clearly she would not become a soloist. But when she was invited to accompany a middle-aged violinist, Jochen Herrmann, on his concert tour to Cincinnati and Chicago, her father refused permission. Was she old enough legally to defy him? Possibly, by then. But who would pay the conservatory bills? Teetering on the verge of a career, she wept in her sister Ruth's arms. It was a long and bitter year.

The following November, armistice was declared but Ruth's husband had not yet been released from service. There were two babies in the narrow apartment overlooking 30th Street Station. She and Ruth were alone that second long, dreary winter. They hung diapers diagonally across the living room. It did not matter that the damp cloths flapped in their faces; no one would come calling. Influenza had broken out everywhere. People stopped going to concerts. Even on brief trips to market, everyone wore a mask. And still the dreaded fevers came.

Her courses suspended, my mother did not receive a diploma from the conservatory. She carried this sorrow with her to the grave. But she did fulfill her mission the following spring. My father burst into her life just as she was playing some Bach partitas at a small party in the neighborhood. Too late for supper, he came noisily through the doorway and had to be shushed until she finished. He later said that he thought she was Miss High-and-Mighty.

I am trying to imagine their courtship, his persistence, taking her for rides in his Stanley Steamer (he claimed it was the very first in Philadelphia). He was worldly, smoked a pipe, visited restaurants and a hotel where there were Wednesday tea dances. He took her to meet his brother, then a law student at the University of Pennsylvania. She was amazed and thrilled by its expansiveness as they wandered the campus. He put his arm around her waist and she did not remove it.

Shades of pretty Polly, they eloped six weeks later. And years later, that was my mother's second sorrow: she never had a wedding. No white veil edged with seed pearls. No bouquet of lilies and baby's breath. And saddest of all, no organ gently sounding the chords of *Lohengrin* to accompany her journey on Papa's arm down the aisle. A long, long aisle, the organ so mellifluous that each time she imagined it, it brought fresh tears to her eyes.

Of course I had the wedding she longed for. Again there had been a war, again against Germany, this time against Japan as well. There was no white satin available for a wedding dress but my mother altered the heirloom one worn in tandem by my two sisters-in-law the year before and the year before that. I carried the bouquet my mother had not carried. I came down the aisle on my father's arm to the strains of *Lohengrin*. My husband-to-be had just been mustered out of the army. It was June; I had just graduated from Radcliffe. He scoured the haberdasheries of New England to find a white coat for the occasion. For trousers, although they were too short, he wore the dark pants of his brother's navy uniform. He also wore his brother's shoes (too tight) as he had no black ones of his own.

Some nights I come awake, certain that I am hearing my mother, dead thirty years, playing the piano in my girlhood home in Germantown. She has closed the parlor doors to mute the sounds coming from her prized Steinway but her fingernails click distractingly on the keys. Her long red fingernails. They announce her status: she does not cook or clean. She plays the piano for her own pleasure. Her sheet music fits inside the piano bench. I, who never got much beyond Every Good Boy Does Fine, inherited her bench full of scores. Mozart, Beethoven, Bach. They were my albatross. I donated them to the local community music school and suddenly felt twenty pounds lighter.

One other thing about my mother. When I was a small child cranky from disappointment or no nap, my mother amused me with a language she called Gobbly. This was well before *gobbledygook* entered the lingua franca. Her Gobbly contained inflections of questions, exclamations, amusement, and horror, all conveyed in an arpeggio of nonwords. She kept it up until I brightened. It occurs to me now that this was a rudimentary poetry, that it connects my life to hers always, that it ran in my veins from the beginning.

The Horses of Childhood

Long ago, I said in a poem:

> Children, I said to my children,
> I am so old I go back
> to the names of the horses that stood in
> the shafts of Freihofer's truck.
> To the milkman's Nelly clopping
> daily, reins loose on her rump,
> her small brain starting and stopping.
> I go back to sugar lumps
> pilfered in careful bunches
> for the junkman's raggedy Bob.
> In the days of all my old horses
> I knew my job.

I have now spent much of my adult life in the company of horses, breeding and raising them, competing with them under saddle and in harness, and today, two years after a nearly fatal carriage-driving accident with my best-of-all horses, I am content to look after just two of the dozen I worked with so closely.

In my parents' generation, before the internal combustion engine, horses provided the locomotion that preceded every means of conveyance we now take for granted. They persisted well into my own childhood. In the Depression, horses were cheaper than trucks. Freihofer's Bakery, in the poem above, dispensed bread, rolls, and coffee cake daily from the back of a closed wagon not unlike the ones still in use among the Amish.

In addition to milk in glass bottles, the dairy wagon drawn by Nelly delivered butter, cream, and eggs. One wintry morning in suburban Philadelphia, I stole two of my brothers' summer camp blankets and ran out to proffer them to the bewildered garbage collector. He agreed to cover the backs of the workhorses that were struggling to pull a loaded wagon up our icy hill.

Before clothes dryers, laundry was pinned to lines out-of-doors and the lines were raised high enough by clothes props to accommodate sheets and other bedding. The same man who toured the neighborhood ready to buy "Junk? Any old junk?" also called out, "Clo's props! Five a dolla clo's props!" He was good-natured enough to put up with a child who ran out every week to greet his horse with expensive sugar lumps, intended for the postprandial coffee tray when guests came to dinner.

I had a silly uncle who promised me a pony every year for Christmas and found my annual disappointment amusing. As soon as I was old enough to leave the block I lived on, I hung out at a livery stable about a mile away. Here, I learned to muck stalls, sweep the aisles, and clean tack. Here, I took my first riding lessons at age ten and earned extra ones through diligence.

I remember the names of all these old horses, too, faithful schoolies who carried inept beginners on their backs. Lacking a ring, we rode down city streets to the park where the instructor, a lead shank attached to the beginner's horse's bridle, taught the student how to post, using his hand under her elbow to raise her up and down in cadence. These undistinguished horses were named Charlie, Monty, Ebony, Slick, and Vixen. By the time the beginner had graduated to Vixen, she was off the lead line and allowed to canter briefly at certain specific points on the trail.

It wasn't much of a life for a school horse then, in a stone stable on a side street just west of a big city, and it was far worse for the dray horses that went out in harness daily in all weathers and came back at evening to straight stalls and small comfort. Horses were routinely underfed so that they wouldn't act up. I was dedicated to remedying this situation with carrots, apples, and sugar treats.

I think this is why I remember their names and faces so clearly, sometimes more clearly than my own equines', the ones I midwifed into this world of privilege and green pastures. If there were a heaven and a chart for those deserving to enter, the names of the horses of my childhood would be at the top.

Homage to Polly Bunting

Mary Ingraham Bunting-Smith, known as Polly from childhood, was president of Radcliffe College for twelve transformative years from 1960 to 1972 and mentor to hundreds of educated women during her professional lifetime. She died in January 1998 at the age of eighty-seven.

The president's house on Brattle Street was almost always open to students. If the porch light was on, drop-ins were welcome. This policy took some getting used to. It established lines of communication across previously inaccessible routes, where commoners and queen had observed rituals of respect from afar laid down generations before. When I was an undergraduate in the distant forties, Ada Comstock seemed a figurehead, and her successor, Wilbur K. Jordan, even more remote, though both had impeccable professional credentials. The college deans were formidable enough. I never met a woman professor or instructor during those years. We addressed our professors and our tutors formally and they replied in kind.

From her first days in office it was clear that Polly Bunting had something more in mind than stewardship. However logical its creation seems today, the Radcliffe Institute for Independent Study, founded in 1961, was her daring contribution to female scholarship of the era. It was renamed the Bunting Institute in 1978 in her honor; the *Boston Globe* called it a think tank for women. It underwent another name change when Harvard subsumed Radcliffe; the Radcliffe Institute for Advanced Study opened its doors to men in 1999. I can only imagine the chagrin Polly Bunting would have felt.

One fall weekend she hosted a picnic for scholars and their families at her summer house in New Boston, New Hampshire. Forewarned to dress down and wear suitable hiking shoes, a dozen of us followed her brisk stride all afternoon through woodlands to a distant beaver pond. Here, she pointed out an enormous lodge under construction. The assorted children in the group were invited to inspect trees the beavers had gnawed through. We were counseled to listen to the red-winged blackbird and the pewee.

On the return trip our eight-year-old son complained that he was tired. "Just walk a little faster," Polly told him. "That's what you do when you're tired. It gets you there sooner."

This zeal to get there sooner led some to refer to her as Mary Baker Eddy Bunting behind her back. What she sought was more than equal opportunities for women; she especially wanted to upgrade the status of those professional women whose careers were on hold while they tended homes and children. The Institute, modestly funded by the Carnegie Foundation and other grantors, provided a stipend and work space to a diverse collection of twenty-two scientists, historians, artists, and poets that initial year. For the creative writer, the grant bestowed legitimacy on an otherwise suspect activity. For example, Anne Sexton's polite lie, "I'm sorry I can't talk to you now; I'm making gravy," gave way to "I'm busy writing a poem."

That premier year brought together a delightful mix of artists, writers, and scholars. Sexton and I were the lucky poets. Barbara Swan and Lois Mirski were the painters, Marianna Pineda the sculptor, Lily Makrakis the historian with whom we forged fast friendships. Soon to follow were Tillie Olsen, Ruth Stone, and Ursula Niebuhr. Since then, the Institute has granted scholarships to more than 1,200 women, many of them eminent in their fields. Many more, perhaps never destined for fame, have taken advantage of the breathing room and prestige the scholarship confers.

I don't remember what we had to eat that day in New Boston at Polly Bunting's table: coleslaw, bologna and cheese? It could have been nightingales' tongues and pheasant under glass for the psychological effect it had on the newly anointed. Polly Bunting, with her unfussy square Dutch bob, her habit of kicking off her shoes when the conversation warmed, her open and unprepossessing demeanor, was as exotic and unexpected as a visitor from outer space.

Radcliffe in the Forties

My grandson is a junior at Harvard. He lives in a suite with three roommates, a private bathroom, two refrigerators, a coffeemaker, a microwave, a TV, and every conceivable device for recording and playing music.

My daughters—Harvard 1971—were the first Cliffies to integrate Harvard houses, drape banners protesting the Vietnam War on John Harvard's statue, occupy University Hall, and receive Harvard diplomas.

I too attended Radcliffe during the war years—World War II, that is. Our class of 1946 was the first to attend integrated lectures in Harvard Yard. Until 1943, Harvard professors had trudged north to the Radcliffe Yard and redelivered the same lecture to a genteel assortment of females-only in Longfellow Hall.

Dorm life was rigidly governed. Weekday parietals for freshmen held us to a 10 P.M. curfew, midnight or an occasional 1 A.M. on weekends. Upperclassmen who had achieved dean's list had more leeway; by senior year, as long as you were on dean's list no curfews applied.

Dinners back then were formal affairs. First of all, we had to wear skirts to the dining room. In thrall to the housemother— usually a widow or spinster of some years—we stood behind our chairs until she entered and took her seat. Invariably, she spoke a few words of grace, a practice I deeply resented even then. I remember one housemother who invited her very deaf brother to dinner whenever the menu was particularly hearty. Down the years, her clarion voice still echoes: "More turkey-lurkey, Harold, dear?"

Biddies, a common but no less affectionate name for the mostly Irish maids in uniform who served each table, also cleaned our rooms. They were our dear friends, mooning over the framed snapshots on our bureaus and mothering us in ways that college students today would find both quaint and politically reprehensible. Since there were no facilities on the premises, laundry was mailed home in cardboard boxes especially designed for this purpose. The front of the box had a reversible address label that slipped into a metal frame. Laundry often came back with a tin of home-baked cookies tucked in the middle.

A work schedule rotated us through kitchen service, mostly scraping plates and scrubbing egg-encrusted spoons before they went into the huge, primitive machines that sent up great clouds of steam as they churned. We also were required to take turns at "bells," answering the phone and buzzing the appropriate floor in search of the caller's designate. Each dorm floor had one telephone booth, two communal bathrooms with showers, and a "smoker" or common room, where idle Cliffies assembled to play bridge, chat, and exhale the tars and nicotines from pack after pack of Kools, Chesterfields, and Lucky Strikes.

Small and Spartan, the rooms themselves were furnished with a cot-width bed, a battered wooden desk with a straight-backed chair, and a bureau of the same vintage. Upperclassmen had access to doubles; the most desirable were corner doubles with two windows.

Cabot Hall, where my roommate and I lived for three years in a cozy double, had a flat roof, ideal for sunning or studying in mild weather. Sometimes four or five of us gathered there to recite poetry we had by heart. In fact, the astonishment I felt as a freshman when I discovered I was not alone in the world with my memory bank of Auden and Yeats, Housman and Millay, has never left me.

Just as we were required to take a semester of Bible and Shakespeare in order to graduate, so too were we obligated to pass a swimming test. Radcliffe's less-than-regulation-size pool, hidden in the basement of Agassiz Hall in Radcliffe Yard, was dank and unappealing. (In fact, I confess I had been seriously attracted to Wellesley College for its state-of-the-art natatorium, which boasted an underwater observation room).

Nevertheless, I earned a dollar an hour as lifeguard at this twenty-yard pool, thanks to my Red Cross certification. I also earned a spot on the swimming team, which I captained my senior year. And I am proud to report that under my tutelage two phobic nonswimmers in my class learned how to propel themselves the length of the pool and back and graduated with me.

My other claim to athletic fame was winning a position as stroke my freshman year. Since crew had never been offered at Radcliffe before, our shell was photographed by the *Boston Globe* as it set out on the Charles River. An enterprising boyfriend of mine at the time wangled a print from the newspaper just before he left to serve in the navy.

Despite the war, Harvard houses still held formal dances after each home football game, and I attended several, with a variety of dates. ("Going steady" was no lighthearted matter in those days; it was to be avoided, as it signified serious marital intent.) These dances were a big deal. Jazz and swing were the dominant themes of the era, played by live bands. We went from jitterbugging to "Chattanooga Choo Choo" to snuggling cheek to cheek to the strains of "Deep Purple."

Afterward, our dates walked us back to our dorms in the quad, a distance that my grandson finds unthinkable today. I find it unthinkable, too, but with our dates' arms around us we gamely picked our way in high heels along the uneven brick walks, holding our floor-length skirts off the paving as best we could. It was too cold to neck outside the dorm for very long; of course, men were denied entrance after hours. Did any of them sneak in, through ground-floor windows, for instance? Doubtless an intrepid few did, even knowing that getting caught meant prompt expulsion for both parties. Somewhere Orwell speaks of how difficult it is to make love in a cold climate. A pity he didn't live to marvel at today's coed living arrangements.

Harvard Square in the forties was crammed with men in uniform: ensigns from the Business School; ASTP—Army Student Training Program—privates who were taking accelerated language courses in anticipation of being sent to Russia or Japan; and junior officers in the signal corps, whose assignments were mysterious. We met these splendid specimens at "Jolly-Ups," parties sponsored by Radcliffe and open to all. Very bland refreshments were served, but these did not deter members of the military, far from home and quite possibly bored or homesick or both, from attending and spiking the punch with a flask or two of gin.

One other Cliffie and I signed up for the ASTP Russian language course; it met six days a week at 8 A.M. in Sever Hall from September to May. On day one, we were force-fed the Cyrillic alphabet in both its print and its cursive forms. Four hours of homework each night were required. By the end of the first week, we were reading children's books; by the end of the second, articles in *Pravda*. We frequently signed out at ten o'clock and walked to the then-truly-midget Midget deli on Massachusetts Avenue, where Al Kagan, its Russian proprietor, hovered over our booth. He pressed free end-of-the-day pastries on us while he helped us untangle the several forms of the verb *to go* in all of its conjugations.

It never occurred to us that we were living in the equivalent of Super 8s while our Harvard counterparts luxuriated in accommodations worthy of the Four Seasons. The fact that we attended

Radcliffe conferred on us a level of superiority unmatched by any other of the Seven Sisters. Forbidden to wear blue jeans to Harvard Square, consigned to rooms the size of a broom closet, chaperoned by all-but-senile housemothers, we were nevertheless Cliffies. And we've never forgotten it.

IDENTITY

Am I a Jewish writer?

I know I feel like a Jewish Calvinist—salvation through grace, grace through good works, no idleness allowed (Bellow says in *Herzog:* "Grief, Sir, is a species of idleness")—and in a solid handful of my poems, my persona as a Jew informs the verse.

Do I feel any desire to rebel against the strictures of being labeled Jewish? No, not that I am aware of. Being a Jew didn't have any bearing on my becoming a poet. The forest of poetry is alive with Jews, male and female. In my short stories and first two novels, now decades out of print, certain Jewish characters are pivotal. As for feeling the strictures of being a woman, definitely in the fifties and sixties, even well into the seventies, I was painfully aware of my second-class citizenship as a poet. I was then, and am now, a feminist. Although the playing field is not yet level, it pleases me to see the strides women have made toward economic and literary autonomy.

In 1957, during one of my mother's visits to our modest house in suburban Boston, we gave a small dinner party in her honor. I was struggling to juggle the care and feeding of three young children with the writing of poetry and the ghosting of medical articles for several busy doctors. Cooking and hostessing came hard, but the evening, I thought, was a great success. Over the soapsuds as we tackled the mountain of dishes, my mother turned to me and asked reproachfully, "Don't you have any good *Jewish* friends?"

I had grown up in a nominally observant family of Reform Jews. We had all attended Sunday School; two of my brothers were bar mitzvahed (the third escaped, I know not how). I was confirmed—there were no bat mitzvahs then—but lapsed almost immediately into agnosticism, which preceded a closet atheism from which I emerged in my twenties.

Within the family there was a tacit understanding that German Jews who had migrated to the States in the 1800s were superior to the latecomers, Poles and Russians who had fled the pogroms of Eastern Europe at the end of the century and beyond.

My mother descended from the superior German rootstock; her grandfather had emigrated from Bohemia in 1848 to escape conscription in Metternich's army. She had married beneath her but she was determined to rise above this fact; no Yiddish expressions were to be spoken in her presence. My father, although born in Philadelphia, had parents who were Old World immigrants, and he sprinkled his conversation liberally with Yiddishisms. Although totally at home in himself, he too clung to the prejudice of his era: he referred to his few good *Christian* friends in just those terms.

When I left home to go to college, all such distinctions dissolved and my life, I felt, started over. Here, friendships sprang up among young women with similar passions: for the first time in my seventeen years I encountered others who were not only poetry enthusiasts but could outquote me. They came from private schools such as St. Timothy's and public schools such as Girls' Latin or Bronx High School of Science. Among them were a few blacks, Hispanics, and a sprinkling of foreign students ranging from diplomat brats to refugees from the war in Europe. Majoring in history and literature, I began to see the virtues in a long, relativistic view of society. Cultures came and went. Rome overrode Greece, but it too waned and ultimately collapsed. Jews were constantly persecuted, with a few noble exceptions. The force of other cultures pressing in on a ghettoized group helped to preserve its uniqueness; no wonder we came to call ourselves the Chosen People.

Am I now a Jewish writer? I am a nonbelieving Jew with a strongly developed Jewish consciousness. I haven't been in a synagogue for fifty years, yet I have whole swatches of the old liturgy by heart. In our family, we observe a kitchen religion. My son lays claim to producing the lightest matzo balls for Seder. My older daughter, whose husband is a Unitarian, observes the High Holidays. My younger daughter's biracial son takes part in Friday evening Shabbat ceremonies at his prep school. I cherish the ceremony, I feel an allegiance to the past but continue to deplore the deep tribal hostilities that organized religions foster around the world. My identity as a Jewish woman is simply one more descriptive epithet that accompanies other labels that adhere to me: poet, equestrienne, essayist, organic vegetable farmer, fiction writer, grandmother, even hermit.

It is perhaps in my poetry that my Jewish consciousness best declares itself. An early poem in rhyming couplets, "Sisyphus," first picks up the narrative thread from my childhood. I grew up in a house on a steep hill in Germantown, a suburb of Philadelphia. Next door stood the Convent of the Sisters of St. Joseph; for the first few years of my education I attended convent school, a paradox that never faded. Wheeling the legless man who begged weekdays at the foot of the hill "up past the Sisters of St. Joe," I was startled to be praised by him as "a perfect Christian child."

> One day I said I was a Jew.
> I wished I had. I wanted to.

This overt declaration of identity turns up again and again in poems.

"Can it be / I am the only Jew residing in Danville, Kentucky / looking for matzo in the Safeway and the A&P?" I ask in "Living Alone with Jesus." At the close of "Young Nun at Bread Loaf," describing foraging together for wild mushrooms,

> Sister, Sister Elizabeth Michael
> says we are doing Christ's work, we two.
> She, the rosy girl in a Renoir painting.
> I, an old Jew.

A somewhat later poem, "In the Absence of Bliss: Museum of the Diaspora, Tel Aviv," opens:

> The roasting alive of rabbis
> in the ardor of the Crusades
> went unremarked in *Europe from
> the Holy Roman Empire to 1918,*
> open without prerequisite
> when I was an undergraduate.

and goes on to examine "twenty-two / graphic centuries of kill-the-jew." Toward the close, the poem asks the question,

> what would
> I die for and reciting what?
> Not for Yahweh, Allah, Christ
> those patriarchal fists
> in the face.

Poetry for me is closest to the bone. I write what I feel. I feel I am a Jew. Godless, but not, I hope, goodless.

II. POETS AND POETRY

The Revision of Emily D.: Notes on "After the Poetry Reading"

AFTER THE POETRY READING

If Emily Dickinson lived in the 2000's
and let herself have sex appeal
she'd grow her hair wild and electric
down to her buttocks. She'd wear
magenta tights, black ankle socks
and tiny pointed paddock boots.

Intrigued, I saw how Emily
would master Microsoft, how she
would fax the versicles that Higginson
advised her not to print to MS
APR and 13th Moon.

She'd read aloud at benefits
address the weavers' guild
the garden club, the anarchists
Catholics for free choice
welfare moms, the Wouldbegoods
and the Temple Sinai sisterhood.

Thinking the same thing, silent
we poets see Emily flamboyant.
Her words for the centuries to come
are pithy, oxymoronic.
Her fly buzzes me all the way home.

"After the Poetry Reading" came in response to poet Marie Howe's whispers countering what seemed, I think, to both of us some tendentious remarks about Emily—Emily, the male poet's refuge. Whenever anyone asked him what women poets he read, he read Emily, long gone and safely dead.

I don't think Emily today would be an activist, alas. I see her living in a remote cottage in Eastport, Maine, or in Vermont's Northeast Kingdom with a big dog and possibly several feral cats she has tamed with time, sardines, and patience. An unknown admirer—woodsy, rugged, and just as shy as Emily—keeps her well supplied with split wood for her stove. Frequently at her back door she finds cornbread muffins or apple turnovers. I suspect she would be computerized, rather secretive about it, guarding her address from the general world, but involved via e-mail with several sister poets, which would relieve her of the considerable onus of having to go to the local post office to send and receive mail. She wouldn't need Higginson in today's world. She might very well be sending her poems to places like *American Poetry Review* and *13th Moon*. Chances are she might have assembled a chapbook by now. She has probably set aside her virginal whites in favor of jeans and lumberjack shirts, clothing in which she feels private, safe, and anonymous. I'd love to see her reading aloud at benefits but I don't think it would be in keeping with her hermetic character. It does seem quite possible that, given the electronic ease in communication available, she might feel freer to express herself, knowing that she was in control of her work at all times. Thanks to her computer she need not suffer fools gladly; unsolicited letters and manuscripts would be starchily returned with a one-sentence note advising the sender of the etiquette of first making inquiry. Or maybe not returned at all.

The poems would be the same, however. Nothing would obtrude on the vivid, unexpected, sometimes oracular language we have come to cherish. My Emily of today belongs as well to yesterday and tomorrow.

On Receiving the Frost Medal

Let me begin by saying that receiving the Frost Medal is especially meaningful to me because I am old enough to have had some personal acquaintance with Mr. Frost—as he liked to be called—at the Bread Loaf Writers' Conference in those August sessions for the lucky few.

And long before that, when I was an undergraduate at Radcliffe in the forties, I had the great good fortune to hear Mr. Frost read on two occasions to overflow crowds in Sever Hall, one of Harvard's largest classrooms. Students wedged themselves into the window wells and stood along the sides and back of the room as the wise old trouper indulged everyone by reciting his crowd-pleasing favorites: "Stopping by Woods on a Snowy Evening," "Acquainted with the Night," "Provide, Provide," and "Birches." He paused to say something between poems, explaining, for instance, how he was forced by the exigencies of the rhyme scheme to repeat the penultimate line, "And miles to go before I sleep," and how he inadvertently locked himself into the dense triplet lines of

> Better to go down dignified
> with boughten friendship at your side
> than none at all: provide provide.

But he was a far more complex individual than the quintessential Yankee farmer-poet so popular with elementary school classes, a crusty old bard with twinkly blue eyes, white hair streaming in the New England breeze. Robert Frost could also mock, convey bitterness, skepticism, or defiance, as in such short lyrical narratives as "Desert Places," "Design," or "Neither Out Far Nor In Deep." But his intent was not directly or specifically political.

I see my own work shifting its focus from the almost explicitly pastoral to poems looking outward, persona poems, poems dealing with the horrific subjects of extraordinary rendition, waterboarding, waiting to be rescued. There was a time when friends teased me with the epithet Roberta Frost, which I took pleasure in. I don't mean to apologize for such poems; if anything, I rejoice in them. The poetry umbrella has to be broad enough to shelter all of us. I would defend to the death the poet's right to be inward, to explore his or her own sensibilities in whatever frame.

But I find I agree with Hans Magnus Enzensberger, who says that the modern-day poet who shuns what we call, perhaps for want of a better term, the "poetic" of our time, does so at great spiritual cost. This is the aesthetics of an elite culture that claims a "good" poem is not political. This is why, to paraphrase Katha Pollitt, we do not have readers—in contrast, for instance, with the poets of Latin America, who have large followings. There, poetry matters. The political scene gives their work impetus and validity. Here, and I quote, "our voices, our power has been taken from us . . . so that at best we are impotent voyeurs of a barbaric and stupid world."

What is the role of the American poet in the nuclear—or "nucular," as the president insists on pronouncing it—age? Why is our response to the menace of global destruction so meager? Partly it seems that the subject is too big, unwieldy, futile. What use are protest poems? They are read only by the already converted, goes the argument. In April, designated as National Poetry Month, poetry gets a polite nod on television. Otherwise, only poets read other poets; they and a sprinkling of academics and eccentrics comprise the audience.

Of course, the poet is not alone in his obscurity. Kurt Vonnegut insisted that writers in America have about as much impact as a pancake falling from a height of four feet. Later, he did admit that if he didn't believe writers had some impact on their times he would have become an optometrist instead. And Arthur Miller said he began to write in the thirties because he found life totally irrational in a world "where people were starving on street corners and we were burning wheat in the west." He sees the writer as an outsider crying aloud, "Life should be better than this!"

The problem seems to be how to deal with the enormity of sensory data bombarding the writer in this torn and ravaged world. Especially and specifically for the poet, I think it is an aesthetic issue: how to deal with the incredible ingenuity of man's inhumanity to man; how to write tellingly and intimately about modern-day acts of depravity so grotesque, so exquisitely cruel, that the deranged Roman emperors and the fifteenth-century Borgias look like mere juvenile delinquents by comparison. How do you make a poem that speaks of social justice when, nightly on television, we are treated to scenes of carnage, eyewitness accounts of rapes and dismemberments, and tortures so extreme that crucifixion would appear by comparison a blessed death?

Czesław Miłosz, who survived the Nazi occupation, spoke to this issue in the Charles Eliot Norton lectures he delivered at Harvard. He recounted the history of Polish poetry, which went underground during the war and was circulated clandestinely. The poetry of the prewar years, which had closely identified itself with European attitudes, was totally lost. What survived were the documentary poems of the Holocaust victims. A new attentive respect to a subject matter far removed from the stylistic mode of the past continues to develop. To transform this material artistically is the challenge.

When Frost proclaimed a bit showily that he had enjoyed a lover's quarrel with the world, it was a safe and secure world. The position of the romantic is that of the individual—intellectually, aesthetically, and emotionally superior to the crowd—whose mission is to prophesy or rail against the stable, ongoing culture he lives in. Today, the poet cannot escape his or her obligation to bear witness. It is impossible to separate the life and the art. Wherever there is language, there too stands the poet, a little to one side, but there. Whether the subject is a diving beetle or a fire bombing, the poet's function is to speak of the encounter.

And now, like the serpent with his tail in his mouth, I would like to close by recalling that Bread Loaf setting I mentioned in my opening paragraph. Shy, insecure, I was nevertheless one of the chosen I refer to in the poem. I am truly grateful for the event, my memory of it, and the special burnish it provides the Robert Frost Medal tonight.

THE FINAL POEM

Bread Loaf, late August, the chemistry
of a New England fall already

inviting the swamp maples to flare.
Magisterial in the white wicker rocker

Robert Frost at rest after giving
a savage reading, holding

nothing back, his rage
at dying, *not yet,* as he barged

his chair forth, then back, his *not yet*
unspoken but manifest. *Don't sit*

there mumbling in the shadows, call
yourselves poets? All

but a handful scattered. Fate
rearranged us happy few at his feet.

He rocked us until midnight. I took
away these close-lipped dicta. *Look*

up from the page. Pause between poems.
Say something about the next one.

Otherwise the audience
will coast, they can't take in

half of what you're giving them.
Reaching for the knob of his cane

he rose and flung this exit line:
Make every poem your final poem.

Brief Speech at the Poetry Society of America's Laureates' Dinner

Now, a brief reprise of my tenure as consultant in poetry to the Library of Congress for eighteen months in 1981 to 1982. Between 1937 and 1981 there had been only four women and one African-American named to the post, now known as poet laureate. "We don't count," the head librarian said to the press when this issue was raised at the luncheon announcing my appointment. "But we do," I replied. And little by little, we counted more. So it is very gratifying to have Louise Glück and, in absentia, Rita Dove sharing this honor with me tonight.

I am happy to say that a number of outstanding women poets, who had not previously been invited, came to read in the monthly events at the Library while I was in the catbird seat. Audre Lorde came, and valiant Josephine Miles. Eleanor Ross Taylor, Ruth Stone, and Lucille Clifton. When Adrienne Rich, who had declined all previous invitations, accepted, the auditorium filled to capacity and closed-circuit TV had to be set up in another venue.

And then there were the brown-bag lunches. I asked a small cadre of local, established women writers in any genre to bring a disciple to the august Poetry Room at noon on Thursdays. Soon our numbers overflowed the lovely antique furniture in this room facing the Capitol, and we sat on the floor with our homemade sandwiches and the cheese and fruit left over from the public reception of the previous night. Calvin, who ran the elevator and helped out in the kitchen, sometimes sneaked leftover wine up to us as well. Twelve to one stretched to twelve to two, then three and beyond.

When I'm gone, I would like to be remembered for instituting the brown-bag lunches.

CELEBRATING JOSEPHINE JACOBSEN, 1997 FROST MEDAL WINNER

Years ago, Stanley Kunitz said something I've always treasured (I am paraphrasing): "Youth is a biological condition, not a state of genius." Conversely, it seems to me, age too is biology; it does not automatically confer grace, virtue, or genius. And those of us who are old or older especially do not want to be reverenced just for lasting.

So the fact that we have sixty years of Josephine Jacobsen's poems contained now in her new and collected volume, *In the Crevice of Time,* is, simply, fact. And while she would not wish bells to be rung or whistles blown merely to recognize her eighty-nine years on earth, in truth her work merits the whistles and bells. I think we cannot sound them loudly enough in praise of this remarkable poet whose dedication to her craft has never wavered. I'd like to quote just a few of her bons mots about the state of being a poet from an interview given to Evelyn Prettyman in 1984:

She said unflinchingly, "I have no interest in a poem which just makes a flat statement and has no countercurrent."

Her poems are rich in countercurrents.

She has said that writing poems is dangerous. "You're starting out on a journey in which you really don't know your destination. The chances are that it's not going to come off, that you're never going to get this nebulous, mysterious thing into language at all."

And yet, over and over, the "nebulous, mysterious thing" has taken shape and moves us.

When asked to compare writing poetry and fiction, she said, "In my heart, there is nothing that compares to poetry. . . . It's like a delicate operation. Under certain conditions you can't go that far in because you get to an organ that is a life source, and I feel that with poetry you get closer to that organ; I feel you're getting in as deep as possible."

Unlike many of us poets who share worksheets of a poem in progress with a trusted poet critic, Josephine Jacobsen eschews such exchanges. For her, the writing of a poem is, in her own words, "an immensely private occupation." And yet, once the poem is made and belongs to the ages, she turns Auden's statement on its head, for she believes that poetry *can* make things happen, though the change is painfully slow. So this very private poet continues to have faith in the public process and while she is not, as she puts it, "kindled by a poem with a purpose," she believes in the poem's ability to move us toward amelioration.

Josephine was born in Canada, spent her early years in North Carolina, and thereafter lived in Baltimore. Her father died when she was five years old and her memories of him are mythic and grand: she remembers scars on his face from fencing and heroic tales of his days as captain of a bobsled team. She was what we would call today "homeschooled." By the time she was sent to Roland Park Country Day School, she lamented that they were done with geography and it had passed her by. To her sorrow she never went to college. Her southern genteel mother felt that college was a refuge for girls who had problems or who didn't have, I am quoting, "a young man on the scene."

Josephine and Eric were married in 1932. I only recently learned that Eric came from a tea-importing family that went back to the days of clipper ships and was a highly regarded tea connoisseur. I was told that not only could he discriminate among the several tea plantations of Ceylon but he could by taste discern on which side of the mountain the tea had grown.

The Jacobsens spent two months a year on the island of Grenada at the same resort, until it was "claimed" in the Falklands War. That landscape figures heavily in Josephine's short stories and to a lesser extent in her poems. We meet mongooses, wild parrots, and lizards; we attend a church healing ceremony.

Summers the Jacobsens moved up to the old frame house in Whitefield, New Hampshire, sometimes driving two cars north in tandem, Josephine valiantly leading, Eric gallantly bringing up the rear so that he could rescue her in the event of mishap. Although there are traces of the New England setting in some poems, Jacobsen was not a traditional poet of place. Her poems are portraits, cameos, ideas, most often lit from within.

Wherever they were, Josephine made time and space for her writing, but she did this so modestly that when you visited you came away with the impression that her sole mission in life was to present a gracious setting in which to entertain friends. Sherry was provided at every lunch and two mighty martinis with a twist preceded every dinner. When she was named consultant in poetry to the Library of Congress, she said of the appointment, which provides an office and staff: "My ultimate place would be a closet. I work better the more I am confined and the less I am distracted."

Harriet Monroe, the founder of *Poetry* magazine, first published Josephine Jacobsen in that magazine, and every editor of *Poetry* from that time forward has printed her poems. Her work has appeared in publications ranging from the *Atlantic* to *Yankee;* the *Nation* to the *New Republic* to the *New Yorker.* It seems to me the most distinguishing aspect of her poems is their clarity. From the very first group dated 1935 to 1950 to the most recent and perhaps most poignant ones, there is a watchmaker's precision to her language, a surgical deftness that cuts to the specifics, and a passion that is controlled but ever pulsing.

I spent some happy hours this week rereading the poems in *In the Crevice of Time.* The leftover academic in me attempted to parse them, as it were, to place them in categories so that students might be told: here are the political poems from the McCarthy period, for example; here are the elegies; over there the love poems; next come the family poems; in this pile the colorful ones about the Caribbean, the ocean, and so on. Happily, this could not be done because of what I will rather crudely call overlap.

One grouping did announce itself: poems about what Lewis Carroll called "reeling and writhing." Josephine can be mordantly funny on the subject of the minor poet, at dinner. We see in perfect iambic tetrameter neatly rhymed how he "sits at meat / with danger smoldering in his eye" and how "by salad time, the very cheese / is paler for his scorn and lore." This same poor dolt reappears in "Birdsong of the Lesser Poet":

> Exuding someone's Scotch in a moving mist
> abstracted as he broods upon that grant,
> he has an intimate word for those who might assist;
> for a bad review, a memory to shame the elephant.

We all know him, do we not? As we know these figures "gathered in inter-admiration / in a small hotel to listen / to each other" in a poem titled "When the Five Prominent Poets":

> When the Muse came,
>
> It was awful.
> The door in shivers and a path
> plowed like a twister through everything.
> Eyeballs and fingers littered that room.
> When the floor exploded the ceiling

THE ROOTS OF THINGS

parted
and the Muse went on and up; and not a sound
came from the savage carpet.

Earned scorn is delicious in the hands of Josephine Jacobsen, but so is praise, as in this poem, "Gentle Reader":

Late in the night when I should be asleep
under the city stars in a small room
I read a poet. A poet: not
a versifier. Not a hot-shot
ethic-monger, laying about
him; not a diary of lying
about in cruel cruel beds, crying.
A poet, dangerous and steep.

O God, it peels me, juices me like a press;
this poetry drinks me, eats me, gut and marrow
until I exist in its jester's sorrow,
until my juices feed a savage sight
that runs along the lines, bright
as bears' eyes. The rubble splays to dust:
city, book, bed, leaving my ear's lust
saying like Molly, yes, yes, yes O yes.

Last in this category, "A Rainy Night at the Writers' Colony," this from her sheaf dated 1970 to 1975, a small narrow poem mostly in trimeter, the quatrains tightly rhymed, a rhythm that always induces in me the delicious melancholy of an A. E. Housman lyric—and I intend that as high praise. I'll just read the first two stanzas.

Dead poets stalk the air,
stride through tall rain and peer

through wet panes where
we sleep, or do not, here.

I know the names of some
and can say what they said.
What do we say worth the while
of the ears of the dead?

This leaves me little time to talk about Josephine Jacobsen's portraitures. She exhibits great sympathy for the old, the confused, the unfortunates of every situation; the mad, the dying, the deaf mutes at a ballgame, the Eskimo woman cooking with heather, lying flat "to cook in a flat hut with a hole / in its roof. Blow! Blow! the ashes flew / into her mane, her red mongoose eyes." And then there are Mrs. Pondicherry and Mr. Mahoney, Mrs. Mobey, the Indestructible Girl of the Carnival, the Night Watchman, the limbo dancer, the blue-eyed exterminator, even the two men lost in the local woods. And a wonderful poem about the garbage collectors, from which I pluck these few lines:

There are things here will go
in the same slam and crash.
Nor will she lie always

on the pillow's fresh surface,
hand curled at her cheek,
and wait for the wondrous

sluice of silence
that carries the blundering
laborious monster,

its unseen men clinging,
who erase time's disasters.
Without moving she lies

while the wings of great scavengers
pass over the roof toward
the hills of discard.

I feel I have not begun to say it, have not mentioned the
poems in which death is subject and predicate, neither to be
feared nor courted. Jacobsen is just as clear-eyed here as elsewhere. And she wants to be accessible, for as she says, "deliberate
obscurity is infanticide for the developing poem." When she
writes about the "first frost of sudden fall," she says that the dead
come into her dreams as "freely as thirst to water"—an amazing
image in this idiosyncratic sestina titled "The Gathering." And
further, on the coming of winter, "The birds/take their lives in
their wings/for the cruel trip . . . Summer is what we had./Say
nothing yet./Prepare."

No obfuscation here. And none in this review of *The Chinese
Insomniacs*, published in the *Washington Post* in 1982, with which
I will close. The reviewer is Carolyn Kizer, who is possibly flam-
boyantly famous for her refusal to mince words: "There is one
further thing about Jacobsen I feel compelled to say, which will
do neither her nor me any good with our formidable sisters: she
is a lady. The dictionaries are not a lot of help here, because, male-
written, they do not mean what I mean, obsessed as they are with
rank and status. Piecing bits together from this source and that,
I define it thus: she is gentle, tactful and incapable of cruelty,
though she understands it well. She is the obverse of innocence,
and more beautiful."

Introduction to *Carolyn Kizer:*
Perspectives on Her Life and Work

Carolyn Kizer was a feminist before the word came into vogue. Her best-known poem, "Pro Femina," legitimized a new generation of women writers with attention to the undisclosed facts of their lives. "I will speak about women of letters, for I'm in the racket," she declares. But "Pro Femina" was merely the curtain-raiser. Her work has steadily grown more political, more worldly, while at the same time preserving the candor and tenderness that illuminate such poems as "Gerda" and "Pearl," in which she writes from the point of view of the child she was, taking refuge in the third person in order to deliver these passionate elegies.

Cheek by jowl are poems about the Alaskan oil spill; the Gulf War; a stunning disquisition on Franco's regime; a deeply moving and tightly knit retrospective about Einstein, Pearl Harbor, Heisenberg, and Hiroshima titled "Twelve O'Clock," in which Kizer seeks to contrast the belief in an orderly universe with the theory of a random, disorderly one. Interspersed among these poems of conviction are less immediately topical ones alight with blinding flashes of satire and sharp humor. One of the best of these arose from a translation of Canto XVII of Dante's *Inferno* that Ecco Press had asked her to undertake. Hers—"In Hell with Virg and Dan"—was deemed irreverent and unsuitable for inclusion in their text, but Ecco's loss is the general public's gain.

Carolyn's mind has the broad range of a predator, the vocabulary of a lexicographer, and the rich lyricism of those songwriters of the forties whom we both adore. Remembering the ways in which our lives intersected has been gratifying.

We were born in the same year, Carolyn an only and late child, I the fourth and only girl in my family. Her ancestors are named and numbered; they reach back to a Dutch Mennonite minister who settled in Germantown, Pennsylvania, in 1690. This beguiles me, for I was born and raised in Germantown, child of another distinctive culture, descended on my father's side from the shtetls of Eastern Europe, and on my mother's from a youth fleeing conscription in Metternich's army in 1848. Carolyn's parents reveled in the precocity and imagination of their prodigy. She was the spoiled darling, the young tyrant, an early reader and memorizer, a playwright and poet at age eight. I too was an omnivorous reader and precocious poet, but introverted, cross-eyed, and shy. Would we have liked each other back then? I strenuously doubt it.

Both of us attended the local public schools, blessed with impoverished but dedicated spinster teachers who loved us. And why not? We were early readers, attentive and eager for more. Both of us noticed the One Good Dress Miss Blomberg or Miss Odell wore three days a week, the Other Good Dress on Tuesdays and Thursdays. This was the Depression; teachers who married immediately lost their jobs.

Carolyn's school drew in equal proportions from middle-class homes, the nearby army post, and a slum area of Spokane. The principal of my elementary school boasted that her population contained no "Negroes"; any who applied were shunted to the adjoining, poorer district.

East and West, Carolyn and I learned all the words and melodies of Stephen Foster's romantic spirituals in our once-a-week music class, and neither of us has forgotten the racist lyrics of "Old Black Joe," "Carry Me Back to Ole Virginny," or "Massa's in de Cold Ground." Carolyn had a fine singing voice; notably deficient in that area, in school I was asked to mouth the words silently.

In 1959, emboldened by acceptances in the *New Orleans Poetry Journal* and *Audience,* both long defunct, I sent poems to a new publication founded by a then-unknown-to-me editor. The magazine was *Poetry Northwest,* the editor, Carolyn Kizer; the poem she accepted was a sestina. Two years later, each of us published a first book.

Destiny didn't actually bring us together until almost a decade later: 1967, in Washington, D.C. Carolyn, the first director of the literature program of the newly founded National Endowment for the Arts, had invited a clutch of poets to read from their work. I remember being escorted that afternoon by someone from the staff to the august Gertrude Whittall Auditorium of the Library of Congress so that the audio engineer could take a voice level. That evening was to be my first experience on so imposing a stage. To add to my terror, a Junoesque woman in a large, stylish hat was overseeing the procedure from the last row of seats. She was entirely at home there, on a first-name basis with technicians, librarians, and poets, calling out suggestions, soothing everyone she addressed.

That was Carolyn. She took me home with her, assuaged my anxiety with a bowl of matzo ball soup (the first time I ever encountered the canned variety, but it's the thought that counts), and thence our friendship began.

All sorts of interesting people gathered in Carolyn's living room in that capacious house in Georgetown, among them the Bengali poet Aijaz Ahmad and John L'Heureux, a former priest who turned first to poetry and then with considerable success to fiction. Carolyn's three quite spectacular teenagers came and went, very much at home in the mélange, much as I now imagine Carolyn herself had been among the assorted lawyers, politicians, and literati of her girlhood in Spokane.

But it wasn't until 1986 that we began to exchange worksheets of our poems. I was in San Francisco visiting a daughter; Carolyn was scheduled to read from her new book, *The Nearness of You,* at the renowned Black Oak Books in Berkeley. We entered arm in arm, singing from that hit song of our college days, "It's not the bright lights that excite me / that thrill and delight me / oh no. It's just the nearness of you." Later, over cocktails, we found ourselves lamenting the dearth of fellow poet-critics. Almost simultaneously it occurred to us that we could be each other's sounding board. There was, we agreed, no mercy to be shown.

From then on, poems crossed the continent to be scribbled on, rearranged, or, in rare instances, simply applauded. One of the poems I earnestly applaud is "Parents' Pantoum," to be found first in *Harping On* and now in *Cool, Calm & Collected.* It is quite simply perfect, proving once again that in the right hands the ancient forms are alive and well.

At the bottom of a worksheet of mine that opens, "The world is awash in unwanted dogs," Carolyn has written, "My dove, you're asking *me* if this is too polemical? I *love* it when you get down and deal with the dirty world." And in reply to a draft of "The Oration," I wrote: "I love this but am troubled by incipient rhymes that then get dropped. I know we have differing opinions here." Often, on the poems themselves, words are crossed out, synonyms suggested, stanza orders are rearranged, better endings are plucked from the middle of the text and held up for scrutiny. There is no substitute for this kind of cross-fertilization and I know that we are not alone in utilizing it.

Letters, too, travel from California to New Hampshire and back at irregular intervals: Carolyn's sometimes typed but frequently in a tidy and readable longhand; mine initially on the IBM Selectric I still treasure, then on my Mac computer. No computers for Carolyn! No e-mail! She will have none of that glib, facile, rat-tat-tat exchange. When there are immediate decisions to be made, or factual information to convey, we communicate by phone, which is somewhat limiting given the three-hour time difference.

Each of us was chosen to join the Board of Chancellors of the Academy of American Poets, Carolyn in 1993 and I two years later. I think we both had reservations from the outset about entering what was clearly The Establishment but we concluded that it was probably a good idea to sign on and try to bore from within to unlock the death grip of the old-boy network. At that time, chancellors were elected to twelve-year terms, renewable once. This quarter-century tenure made for a rock-hard board ruled by what Fred Viebahn was to call, in his letter to Stanley Kunitz, by then chancellor emeritus, "this unabashed country club mentality."

Our qualms were magnified when James Merrill's death created an opening on the board, and candidates to fill the position were to be nominated by the chancellors. Each of us, without prior consultation—I think Carolyn was on the road giving poetry readings at the time—proposed Lucille Clifton. She did not make the cut. We were outvoted by a sizable majority. The following year, when a chancellor came to the end of his second twelve-year term and departed from the board, there was once again an opportunity to lobby for Lucille to fill the vacancy. Once again a white male poet was elected instead.

The decision to resign was arrived at independently over the fall of 1998. Still suffering chronic pain from my nearly fatal carriage-driving accident that July, I just didn't feel up to the task of protest. As I remember it, I called Carolyn and told her I wanted out. She then said, "Well, you can't just go quietly. We have to stick together and resign at the exact same time."

I agreed that our renunciations needed to count for something. We tendered our resignations, along with individual letters stating our reasons, by faxes, coordinated to allow for the three-hour time difference, copies to follow by U.S. mail. We cited the German writer Fred Viebahn's initiative in his essay, "Unmasking the 'Gods of Poetry,'" accusing the board of persistent racism. Viebahn, husband of black poet Rita Dove, a former U.S. poet laureate, had taken his argument to *Poets and Writers,* where it had evoked strong support on the one hand and considerable fury on the other. Two senior members of the Academy of American Poets attacked him in its pages for his "destructive, polarizing rhetoric," and when Viebahn sought to respond, the editors informed him that his rejoinder would not be printed. The full text of this literary joust, reported by Charles H. Rowell, can be seen in *Callaloo* 22.1 (1999). I have also discussed it further in the recorded version of my keynote address to the members of PEN–New England in April 1999 in *Always Beginning.*

Afterward, I was relieved that it was over, but it turned out that it had hardly begun. It was Carolyn who took hold, phoning Harvey Shapiro at the *New York Times* to inquire if our posture was newsworthy. He declared that it was indeed, and one of the *Times*'s top byliners, Dinitia Smith, was assigned the story.

Smith's article, which appeared in the *Times* of November 14, 1998, cited the following statistics: "Since the academy was founded [by Marie Bullock in 1934] there have been 57 chancellors. Twelve women have been elected, but there has never been a black chancellor." She went on to quote Jonathan Galassi, president of the academy and editor in chief of Farrar, Straus and Giroux, who "said of the resignations of Ms. Kumin and Ms. Kizer: 'I was very sorry that they are doing this at a time when we are in the process of putting our governing structure through review.' He said that he would not accept the resignations and that he would try to persuade both poets to remain as chancellors to help him make changes at the academy."

This conversation never took place. Carolyn was hopeful that we would be reinstated but I knew better. We were not.

I don't think either of us expected quite the coverage our resignations were accorded. We made some enemies but the ones we made, I think, are worth having. Today, the Academy of American Poets boasts a multicultural Board of Chancellors, including, at this writing, not only Lucille Clifton but also Yusef Komunyakaa and Jay Wright. The length of office has been reduced—no more quarter-century tenures—and the entire organization has acquired a benign sparkle.

As for Kizer and Kumin, our old friendship endures, coast to coast. I take to heart her final dicta from "Fin-de-Siècle Blues": "Call up Voltaire. Tend the garden. / Seize the day."

KIDDIELIT WITH ANNE SEXTON

Today I sat down and revisited four children's books that Anne Sexton and I wrote collaboratively and often with great hilarity, beginning in 1963 with *Eggs of Things,* a See and Read science title published by G. P. Putnam's Sons. Our seventeen-year friendship was initiated in 1957 when we met in a poetry workshop at the Boston Center for Adult Education and decided to carpool each week from the suburb where we both lived. We remained intimate personal and warm professional friends until her suicide in 1974.

But what were serious poets doing, thinking up plots for kiddielit, as it was dismissively known in the trade? Weren't we scribbling furiously into the night to create real poems—"real toads in imaginary gardens," as Marianne Moore had insisted? We were. Daily, over the second phone line we had had installed in our houses so we could stay connected as long as we wanted, we read our poems in process to one another. Although by 1963 we had each published a first book, we were hungry for further recognition in the largely male domain of letters. Our poetry world was gradually expanding and we worked diligently to enlarge our individual places in it. But on the side I had begun writing children's books in 1959 for our own bedtime audience. Putnam published my first try—*Sebastian and the Dragon*—the following year. Suddenly I had what then seemed a substantial check—$500—and a welcome invitation to write more.

Eggs of Things was to be my eighth book with Putnam, several employing the limited vocabulary required for their Beginning to Read series. I enjoyed this challenge so much that I not only wrote four seasons books to order, but chose to write them in verse. Anne was intrigued by this aspect of what we both viewed as high sport for wordsmiths and we agreed to try out our joint skills (in prose, however). Putnam See and Read Books—and now I am quoting from the ponderous dictum provided on the back jacket—"are written with a controlled vocabulary. [They] use those words that children are taught to read in the first grade . . . In addition, the See and Read Books introduce a carefully selected group of new key words based on the specific subject matter in each book. [These books] are fun for children from six to eight, who will enjoy the sense of accomplishment that comes from reading all by themselves."

I seem to remember there was a limit to the number of new words we were allowed to introduce—was it ten? Or twenty? At any rate, the trick was to use words on the already approved list in somewhat unusual ways so that we could save up the new key words as needed—not unlike writing a poem, where compression acts to intensify feeling. The list already had *eggs; things,* too, was one of the acceptables. The title was a natural.

In early spring a year before, my son had captured a scoopful of tadpoles, which he raised in my blue enamel canning kettle. He refreshed them daily with water and plant matter from the local shallow pond until they developed hind legs, and under strong parental suasion he agreed to return them to their original habitat. This provided the mainspring of the story.

As for characters, we agreed on two boys who lived next door to each other. Since *buzz* and *skip* were both allowables, we seized them for names. Of course there had to be a little sister, and *pest*—probably there in some earlier context of *garden, buzz,* and *bee*—instantly attached itself. For the family dog, *cowboy,* which possibly migrated onto the list of permissibles from an earlier book by a Putnam author titled *The Cowboy Surprise,* sounded suitably rakish. Since we were both women poets struggling for recognition in an era dominated by male poets, it was no accident that we gave Pest all the answers in *Eggs of Things:*

> "Why are they bumpy and dry?" asked Pest. "Frogs are smooth and wet."
> The boys didn't know.

It wasn't just a case of gender rivalry. Age mattered too. Small outwitting big drives this plot in which toads save the families' joint vegetable garden, besieged by bugs.

A year later, in its sequel, *More Eggs of Things,* the proceedings are slightly more complicated, but once again, Pest prevails: "Those eggs of yours are not sea gull eggs or duck eggs. Birds' eggs are hard. These eggs are soft."

Not only do they hatch into turtles, but they're endangered ones. That word wasn't in common use in 1964. In *More Eggs of Things,* Pest's friend, Mr. Silver (name on the approved list), who runs a sort of rehabilitation center on the ocean—the sign in the picture says "Ocean Zoo"—gets to say, "These are real treasures, kids . . . These are the first green turtles I have ever seen on this coast . . . Once our ocean was full of them. Now there are not that many left." Excerpted, this sounds preachy, but in the mélange of an ocean storm that strands Cowboy on an island offshore with Candy (also approved), a rescued seal whose pen had been destroyed, action quickly overtakes didactics. Candy sleeps in the old tub used for Cowboy's baths, and a picture of the entire peaceable kingdom makes the front page of the newspaper.

I confess we churned these first two books out in two days. Certainly, having small children must have helped us regress to the psychological level of first graders. We agreed that whoever sat at the typewriter as we composed had, as it were, power of attorney. We alternated at intervals dictated by breaks for coffee, child crises, or phone calls. It was, quite simply, fun.

We were not alone. T. S. Eliot's *Old Possum's Book of Practical Cats,* written in the 1930s, might be thought of as establishing the precedent. Some thirty years later, Randall Jarrell's *The Bat-Poet* received great acclaim. Donald Hall followed with a broad assortment of titles for children, including his hugely successful *Ox-Cart Man,* the proceeds from which built a new wing on the old house at Eagle Pond Farm. X. J. Kennedy, Gwendolyn Brooks, Richard Wilbur, and others also wrote for young audiences. While there were instances of close collaborations between writer and illustrator of children's books, I can't think of any that took place between poets. Certainly none to match the two poets in the Sexton swimming pool on a steamy July day in 1970 taking turns at the typewriter balanced on the pool's outer rim. Six years had elapsed between collaborations, but only because our follow-up sequel, *Cowboy and Pest and the Runaway Goat,* had, after considerable hemming and hawing, been rejected by Putnam. Now we were free to take off in a different direction for a different publisher.

Joey and the Birthday Present, published by McGraw-Hill in 1971, was inspired by the brief life of Anne's daughter Joy's pet mouse. The circumstances of its arrival are now murky; I remember thinking that one mouse in a cage would die of loneliness, which, alas, proved prophetic. Joy's grief was acknowledged in the dedication.

I take credit for the setting, a deserted old farmhouse in the country, not dissimilar from our own, haven for a vast tribe of mice, into which a city family with an old dalmatian moves for the summer. The little boy has a pet white mouse in a cage that he received for his birthday. Joey, a common field mouse whose grandfather was eaten by a cat belonging to an earlier tenant, watches their arrival. Never having seen a cat, he whispers his description to the others: ". . . his terrible toenails click when he walks. His tail is as thick as a chair leg and it thumps from side to side."

Freed from the strictures of a limited vocabulary, we enlarged upon the story of Prince, the white pet-store mouse, and Joey, the brown country mouse who befriends him, and their relationship with the little boy in whose pocket they frequently ride. Nightly, Joey introduces Prince to the indoor joys of exploring between the walls of the house, racing through the attic, and skating around on an overlooked can of bacon fat. Next come the pleasures of outdoor life, where Prince "eats his first dried raspberry and his first mosquito."

The denouement occurs when Joey, who wedges the cage door open every night with a crayon, offers Prince the chance to run away with him rather than return to the city in September. Which of us came up with the key line, "And they both agreed that a birthday present could not run away," neither of us could remember, but I do know that many of the liveliest inventive details were Anne's. It was a lark to collaborate on this sweet tale with a mildly melancholic ending.

We were both considered reputable poets by then. Anne had already won the Pulitzer Prize for her fourth collection. I had published three collections of poems and two novels. While we were still the sounding boards for each other's poems, we once again renewed our collaboration on another, even more fanciful children's story. *The Wizard's Tears,* again with McGraw-Hill, was again illustrated by Evaline Ness, whom we greatly admired, especially for her rendition of dalmatians.

This time, the venue is the mythical village of Drocknock where the old wizard has lost his magical powers and everyone, including the mayor, is covered with chicken pox bumps. Twenty cows are missing from farmer Macadoo's barn and the town reservoir is drying up from the summer's drought. The old wizard decides it is time to retire.

Enter the young wizard, the ink on his diploma barely dry. The wizard encyclopedia provides him with the proper incantations to cure chicken pox and find missing cows—here, Anne shone as she blithely supplied the magical non sequiturs, "WATCH THE MOON OVER YOUR SHOULDER, CATCH A BEE IN A JAR, AND WASH YOUR FACE WITH BUTTERMILK." However, the young wizard is unable to call forth rain to restore the reservoir. He needs five of his own tears to end the drought but he is too happy in Drocknock to cry. Consulted, the old wizard suggests that he peel an onion, but warns him that a wizard's tears are very powerful.

As a result of the tears he manages to bring forth, it rains. The drought ends. The citizens are ecstatic. But the young wizard fails to heed his mentor's warning. Were we thinking of Icarus? Careless with his vast supply of onion-induced tears, the young wizard orders breakfasts in bed that begin with orange juice and end with chocolate cake. Chaos ensues. At this point we were giddy with invention: the entire population of the town, including the mayor and the water commissioner, turns into frogs—perhaps a carryover from the frogs that starred in *Eggs of Things.*

Consulted again, the old wizard poses a riddle, assuring his young protégé that the answer awaits him right before his eyes. His first two guesses fail. On the third and final try the young wizard succeeds in undoing the spell, and the frogs turn back into people once more.

Sadly, Anne did not live to see our happily-ever-after tale come into print in 1975. She took her own life on October 4, 1974, only a few months after we had sold our story to McGraw-Hill. Deprived of the companionship of our collaboration, I put kiddielit aside for almost ten years until a publisher plucked a poem I had written many years earlier and turned it into a little book, *The Microscope,* illustrated by the late Arnold Lobel. It went on to star on PBS's *Reading Rainbow* series. Now Candlewick Press is about to reissue *What Color Is Caesar?,* very slightly rewritten from the McGraw-Hill text of 1978, and Roaring Brook Press will soon publish *O Harry*, a horse story I wrote for my grandson twenty-one years ago when he was six. *O Harry* is in rhyme; it was rejected several times by publishing-house screeners because it employs enjambment, and young children, I was advised, are not capable of making the wraparound leap enjambment entails as they read. Apparently, in the twenty-first century they can.

Cats in Zanzibar

As Henry David Thoreau said, "it is not worth the while to go round the world to count the cats in Zanzibar" in search of yourself. "Extra vagance!" he proclaimed, nailing down the Latin roots of the word he calmly broke in two. "It depends how you are yarded."

Pobiz is both *extra,* "beyond," and *vagant,* "wandering." Composing the poem itself is a separate and self-rewarding process. Traveling around the university reading circuit, the library chain, the prized venues of the Writer's Voice, the 92nd Street Y, the Library of Congress; doing a stint as poet-in-residence at East Geopolis College; conducting workshops; serving on panels at literary conferences—this is the poetry business.

At this writing pobiz appears to be in good health. But consider the homely details of life on the road. It's a little like a life in sales. Lots of flights on little planes out of an airline's hub. Lots of uncertainties, not only about how you will be received but where they'll put you up, who'll turn out for the reading. Who's in the front office, so to speak. Whether you'll hit it off.

Sometimes things go smoothly, as crisply as an iron nosing along the sleeve of the poet's shirt. Planes are met; interviews are conducted tactfully; meals, with a reasonable range of choices, are provided. Sometimes it is otherwise. For example:

I arrive just shy of midnight at the pleasant campus of a middle-sized college and am shown to my room-and-bath on the second floor of a charming old Victorian building. It's a frosty night. The room is stifling but both windows glide open at a touch. There's a coffee machine, a small fridge with milk and orange juice, a bowl, a box of cereal: ideal. I sleep the sleep of the seasoned sojourner . . . and wake to a deeply chilled room. The forced-hot-air blowers of last night are no longer emitting.

There's a phone number for the housekeeper, who has an apartment on the first floor, but no one answers. I leave a polite message and proceed to get dressed for the out-of-doors indoors. When a welcoming member of the faculty calls me shortly after, I explain the situation. She is aghast; she will call Maintenance at once.

It's a Sunday. Abbott and Costello from Maintenance arrive. The thermostat is situated at the top of the second-floor stairs, but its plastic cover is locked in place. After a fruitless thirty minutes trying to insert a screwdriver, a knife, a coat hanger—anything!—in the narrow gap between cover and wall in order to nudge the dial up ("Dammitall, I almost had it" "No, lemme try"), they depart.

Meanwhile, I've discovered an electric baseboard heater with its own thermostat in the bathroom, which I push up to eighty degrees. I assemble breakfast and arrange it on the vanity, manage to wedge the desk chair into the bathroom, close the door behind me, and eat, sitting catty-corner between toilet and sink. The rest of the morning passes deliciously as from under the bedcovers I watch an exercise class on TV, followed by a garden show and a home makeover. (It is too cold to hold a pen, I tell myself.)

A little past noon, Patricia from the faculty arrives to take me to lunch. We walk to the one hotel as nothing else is open on The Lord's Day. Service is slow. Also, we find lots to talk about, so it is midafternoon when we return to campus. The housekeeper is in. She comes upstairs with us and, after several tries, unlocks the cover. The minute she eases the dial upward, the blowers whoosh on in my room.

The reason the cover is locked, she explains, is to prevent guests from tampering with it. I try to visualize naughty guests—children?—pushing the thermostat up and down. The problem, she continues, is that the back rooms, one of which is mine, are the last to get heat. It's a vintage building. It's an issue they plan to deal with. But she agrees to leave the cover off for the remainder of my visit, and I promise not to abuse the privilege.

Indeed, be careful what you wish for. In half an hour my room is too tropical to bear. I tiptoe down the hall and nudge the dial down until the blowers shut off, confident that I can turn them back on at will. After the requisite dinner with faculty and sponsors of the program, after the reading and the book signing, Patricia and a few friends see me to my quarters. The thermostat cover is still absent. My room is only slightly cool; I fall asleep secure in the knowledge that tomorrow morning I can reheat it. After breakfast I will participate in a question-and-answer session and then depart.

When I wake up, the room is once again freezing. I slip down the hall in my nightgown, but wait! The cover is back on, locked in place. I sigh and repeat yesterday's procedure—breakfast in the john again.

A week later, I go to a well-known liberal arts college in a northern state. This gig begins auspiciously. Ralph, the student meeting my plane, stands where we agreed to meet. He's hired a car to convey us from the airport to the college. Of course, there's horrendous traffic. The driver disapproves of Ralph's Mapquest directions and takes his own route. We arrive with an hour to spare, but wait! The key to the guesthouse must be sent for from the building across the quad. Ralph, a meticulous if not obsessive individual, says he fears he will have a nervous breakdown before the key arrives. Even though I am anxious to get settled, I can't say what I really think: why couldn't this detail have been taken care of in advance? Instead, I have to comfort him.

We finally gain entry by way of a Roman-numeraled code. Ralph carries my bags to another suspiciously isolated room and roots around for a door to the bathroom. Mercifully, there is one. No phone, however. There's also a defunct TV, perhaps left in place for decoration, but no matter. I inquire about libations to accompany the buffet supper being set up downstairs and send Ralph off with sufficient funds to purchase a couple of bottles of wine. Three wonderful women faculty members and two glasses of Pinot Grigio revive my flagging spirits.

A packed reading, lots of Q-and-A, lots of books sold and signed. I sleep the only slightly troubled sleep of a poet who cannot make or receive a phone call and is to share the lone bathroom with unknown others. In the morning, just as I am shuffling into my slippers, one unknown but blatantly male other takes possession, sliding the bolt shut just behind my head. Thirty minutes of dramatic hawking and spitting, nose blowing and breaking wind, precede the sounds of shaving, razor rinsed and rapped dozens of times against basin (is he unburdening himself of a lifetime beard?), followed by a greedy shower.

My bladder is bursting. The seemingly endless ablutions end. He remembers to unlock the door to my room.

I endure a lone breakfast in a distant all-but-vacant cafeteria and cross back to the guest house, but I am unable to regain entry. I must go back to cafeteria, halloo into the kitchen, and ask to be rescued. A directional dyslexic, I have transposed the V and the III. A humiliating episode but surely not the last.

At noon, my transport to the next college arrives. We drive to a small town in an adjoining state, where I am to stay in a highly recommended B and B. This young professor claims that many Important Poets before me have stayed there and have given it very high marks. Although he personally has never been there, I am in for a treat, he assures me.

This B and B is a bit off the beaten path. We drive around for what seems hours. When we finally find it, the gates are locked. Honking the horn does not bring a welcoming wave. We get out of the car, precariously parked in a narrow verge, and trek in through a footpath. I circle the property, which clearly was once a grand estate but looks rather shabby from the rear. It sports what my mother used to call a Queen Anne front and a Mary Ann behind. All doors are locked, though one has a note pasted to it welcoming someone named Harris. No note for Kumin. No key. My escort calls on his cell phone and receives a hearty generic we're-away-from-the-phone-just-now message.

By now it is midafternoon. He calls other faculty members but is unable to reach any of them. I suggest a motel, any motel at this point. There is nothing decent, he claims, within a reasonable radius. I stand my ground. We cannot wait for the absent landlords any longer. Finally, he remembers an old inn about twenty miles north and calls information for the number. Yes, they have a vacancy.

At sundown I am settled in a room in a circa-1880 inn. The private bath retains the old white hexagonal floor tiles I remember from my childhood. The same massive fixtures—and the same low water pressure. The floors creak above and below my room when anyone passes, a reassuring sound from my childhood in a similarly somewhat shabby old Victorian.

The reading goes well; there are a few questions, a successful book signing. I am taken out to dinner by two of the English faculty, who bring in a nice bottle of Chardonnay, and eat heartily and appreciatively on the college budget. A check is produced as I say my farewells. A car will come for me in the morning and it does. Not a bad ending.

Perhaps it is here, between gigs, that I remember something else Thoreau had to say, tinged with his New England asperity. He advised the British poet-wannabe that instead of first seeking his mercantile fortune in India, he should have gone up garret at once. The life of hermit-transcendentalist, composing poems in solitude and poverty, indeed has its attractions.

But then there follows a pleasant week at a small red-brick college in Virginia, once known as a finishing school for debutantes, now a multicultural institution. The hotel is only a hundred steps from campus and it offers generous sit-down breakfasts. The faculty members, Ph.D.s from the likes of Emory and Yale, cosset me shamelessly. My husband goes with me on this jaunt. There's the obligatory reception (coat and tie for Victor, a rare occurrence), a reading, several classes to visit. While I teach, he tours Monticello, Appomattox, the Natural Bridge, the Woodrow Wilson Library, and the George C. Marshall Museum.

We are able to free up an afternoon to visit our friends, novelist and essayist Donald McCaig and his wife, Anne, their eighty sheep, and assorted sheepdogs. It's lambing season on the McCaig farm; I'm surprised by this news. In New England, the ewes lamb in late February. This flock, Rambouillet crossed with Tunis, breeds at any season. We get a grand tour of the newborns.

Later, Donald goes out to check on a pregnant ewe he had segregated earlier and returns, carrying the lamb in a sort of harness/cradle that he holds with one hand. The ewe follows, nosing her baby. The sheepdog follows the ewe, nosing her tail stub to guard against any sudden moments of panic. This newborn is a big singleton; when there's a pair, he carries two such harnesses. I ask him what he does if the ewe delivers triplets. "Yell for Anne," he replies.

Later, Donald treats us to a stellar performance: the dog he will take to a show the following weekend herds a flock of about sixty sheep toward us, circles it, divides it in half, reunites the two halves, and takes them back to their original grazing grounds. All this on minimal hand signals and brief whistles. To us it appears a species of magic. This show alone is well worth the long drive over the mountain and back, to say nothing of the last twelve-point-eight miles of rackety gravel road.

A week later, I fly to Kansas City, happy to have found a direct flight from New Hampshire, with one stop in Philadelphia. It is late evening when we land; I am astonished to find my host waiting for me at the gate. Security in Kansas City is minimal;

there is no barrier between deplaning passengers and their welcomers.

I am housed in a small European-style hotel with all the amenities, including breakfast buffet-style downstairs. David takes me to lunch in the atrium of the Nelson-Atkins Museum of Art, a massive open space with three stories' worth of balconies, and provides a brief tour of the city. I remember from a previous visit how delightful the Henry Moore sculptures look, looming over wide green lawns, and how much Kansas City reminds me of Washington, D.C., with its casual open public spaces and its dearth of high-rise buildings.

A young poet on the faculty has arranged a potluck supper at her house before the reading. We move seamlessly from good wine and vegetarian casseroles to the university theater. A full house. Lots of books for sale. The perfect gig, I say to myself, thanking my hosts, who cordially deliver me to the airport in the morning. And it is, until we land in Philadelphia.

There will be a change of equipment here, we are told. The chaos of disembarkment, transfers, and reloading onto another plane ensues, where, after a forty-five-minute hold, the pilot regretfully informs us that our landing strip is fogged in. We cannot take off. Eighty-two stalled passengers once again dumbly disembark. We wait in line like sheep to be rebooked by a single harried agent.

In the meantime, I've struck up a conversation with a couple in their fifties accompanied by two white-haired ladies. They live in the next town over from mine. (That's how we talk in New Hampshire.) We discover we have mutual acquaintances. After we are finally provided with boarding passes for the 10 P.M. flight, we agree to go to the nearest beanery, half bar, half deli, for some supper.

I offer to buy everyone a drink. The middle-aged couple demurs and settles at a table, but the two seniors accompany me to the bar and the three of us hoist ourselves up on stools. One tells me she is eighty-seven, the mother of the man at the table. Her companion and best friend is eighty-five.

The bartender makes a great show of polishing the wood in front of us. We are his only customers.

"What'll you have, ladies?"

"Do you have Tanqueray gin?"

"Yep."

"I'll have Tanqueray gin on the rocks with a twist," declares my neighbor, hitching her stool closer to the bar, and her partner orders the same. I choose a Bloody Mary. After that round, we agree we deserve another go.

The airport gradually empties. The corridor to the ladies' room has grown spookily dim. None of us feels much like talking now. We are the last flight into New Hampshire, arriving just before midnight.

Some months later, I fly south to do two gigs back-to-back. This has been carefully orchestrated in advance. An acquaintance from the first university will meet my flight and convey me seventy miles to my destination. My plane lands in a huge airport. A train connects the several concourses with ticketing and baggage claim. I arrive as agreed at the latter where, on the other side of a token rope barrier, families, friends, and drivers for various limo services are clustered.

I search the lineup anxiously. Sam is not there. To the young man at my right elbow I must appear elderly and bewildered (neither far from the truth), for he offers me the use of his cell phone. Sam has said that he will keep his on just in case. I dial. A female voice picks up quite abruptly: "This is Jane." And then the connection fades. Jane, I think to myself. Jane who? Did I get a wrong number? My companion shows me how to press redial. This time, I have my wits about me. Perhaps this is Sam's wife, whom I have never met. "Is this Jane X?" "Yes. Sam's car broke down halfway to the airport, he had to call me to come get him. We're on our way, about forty minutes to go."

The airline, I learn, had promised to page me but did not. We pass Sam's broken-down car on the other side of the highway. A little after 11 P.M. Sam delivers me to my hotel room, a hospitality suite complete with microwave, refrigerator, sink . . . but no hospitality. No welcoming bowl of fruit and cheese, no crackers. Ah well. This is pobiz, I tell myself.

A moment after he leaves, I realize there is a noisy party taking place next door. Just behind my bed, for that matter. The front desk, confiding that the hospitality suites are always noisy, relocates me to a normal room down the hall.

The next morning I wait anxiously for a call from a friend who lives three hours away and has driven to town for our rendezvous. We plan to have lunch. Each time I call the number of the house where she is staying, I get the answering machine.

At almost noon my door opens. A large gentleman with two suitcases stands there. We are equally bewildered. He starts back to the elevator and I phone the front desk. Not only is the clerk sorry for the error but it appears that a lady—to whom he confesses he gave the wrong room number—has been waiting for me in the lobby for over an hour.

The next morning, a Lincoln Town Car conveys me to a little college with spacious grounds, meticulously tended. An impressive equestrian facility. Herds of free-ranging deer. Paradisiacal. I am shown to my room in one of the college's ancient little guesthouses—once again it has a connecting bath but I am assured no one will share it.

In addition to its antiquity, this accommodation is Spartan. No luggage rack. Three wire hangers. Bare floors. No radio or television. No shelf, table, or stool in the bathroom for toiletries. No complimentary toiletries, needless to say. Supper, alas, served in the college dining room, is dry. I am cross to have to forgo a glass or two of wine but the reading, I am mollified, is packed (I find out later that attendance was mandatory) and there are books for sale.

On the two-hour trip next morning to the airport for my flight home, I lean back in the commodious town car and recall some gigs from long ago. At the now-defunct Eisenhower College in an upstate New York cow pasture, I was shown to a narrow dormitory room with the bath at the end of the hall. It was, at least in my memory, winter and I had neglected to pack bedroom slippers.

Another winter, this time in upstate Maine, housed after the reading in a cozy, electrically heated university apartment overlooking the parking lot, I woke to an unanticipated raging blizzard. It was a real nor'easter. I could barely make out the turtled outline of my car. The entire town had lost power; consequently, there was no heat. The room gradually grew so cold that I took the rug off the floor and covered the bed with it. It is said that freezing to death is not unpleasant. I prepared to find out.

In midmorning, through a peephole I had scraped in the frosted window, I spied a large hooded and booted figure approaching. It was poet Wesley McNair, who had sponsored the event and had assured me the day before that only light snow was predicted.

Fortunately, the McNair homestead was only a few blocks away. Wes hoisted my carry-on to his shoulder and we followed his footsteps back, he in the role of Good King Wenceslas and I the good slave, to the comfort of a woodstove and candlelight. I became Wes and Diane's houseguest for the next forty-eight hours. What luck to fall into such good company! What an unlikely way to initiate a warm friendship that has endured.

Long ago, in Missoula, Montana, when Richard Hugo was still alive, I read at the university at his invitation. Afterward, his wife hosted a barbecue in their spacious backyard. Her two quarter horses wandered around unfenced, like large dogs. Somebody had brought his guitar and we sang a while. I did not know then how little time was left to Dick, only the sweetness of the occasion.

Some years ago, in a small town in the Midwest, I spent several weeks conducting two fiction and poetry workshops at the local college. Here, I was luxuriously housed. I was met and conveyed to every event. Faculty members took turns inviting me to bountiful suppers. I met their dogs and cats and children. Everyone seemed to live in a huge mid-nineteenth-century Gothic house paneled in warm oak, with high ceilings and a third-floor turret. Owners vied with each other to trumpet how inexpensively their houses had been bought.

An air of spaciousness extended to the classes as well. Students here were reasonable and mannerly; it was before body piercing but after sexual liberation. Everyone called the poet by her first name. Comments in the workshops were chummy and direct. Many of the stories were wildly obsessed with sex, both hetero- and homo-, vividly explicated. Some of this, I thought, surely must be invention. They can't all be copulating in these bizarre settings and positions? And then the light dawned: sex had taken the place of political action.

How often, in the course of conducting pobiz, I have met women to admire. Brilliant women scholars teaching in colleges that offered little intellectual stimulation. Wives locked in commuter marriages because neither institution would hire the other spouse, catching the red-eye on one coast or the other on alternate weekends. Soccer-mom professors bonding to pursue outside interests ranging from ornithology to mountain climbing, babies in Snuglis on their backs, toddlers by the hand. Lesbian couples getting together for Saturday night potlucks and poetry workshops in a small college town in the middle of a flyover state.

And then, twenty years ago, I was met by a young woman I'll call Cathy, adjunct professor at a big southwestern university, whom I cannot forget. We set out from the airport in her pickup truck. As we cruised along the interstate at seventy m.p.h., a tire blew. The car behind us barely managed to pull past us without

76   THE ROOTS OF THINGS

incident and sped on. Cathy wrestled the truck to a stop in the deep gravel of the shoulder, but not without damaging the tire rim so that it would not take a spare.

Dame Fortune had arranged to have an exit ramp at that exact spot. We coasted down it to an intersection bounded on all sides by cornfields, where—I swear I am not making this up—a fully operational public telephone booth stood. (Need I explain that this was before cell phones?) Cathy had to make several calls before she was able to reach someone at the poetry festival who was free to come collect us.

In the long afternoon that elapsed before our ride arrived, I learned that her mother, in her late forties, was dying of Huntington's chorea, a hereditary degenerative disorder that results in abnormal writhing and dementia. It is invariably fatal. Children of an affected parent have a fifty percent chance of developing the disease. Predictive testing is available but Cathy hadn't been able to bring herself to undergo it. Meanwhile, she taught freshman comp three days a week and wrote poems she showed to no one. Her husband, spooked by her possibly bleak future, was divorcing her.

I carry Cathy around with me. Why didn't I make the effort to stay in touch with her? Couldn't I have asked her to send me poems? Couldn't I have gradually won her over, gotten her to take the test so as not to live out her life in fear and depression? And if the test was positive, wouldn't she need all the support she could get? Why wasn't I part of that picture?

Pobiz also involves, because of my history of horse connections, visits to barns ranging from elegant facilities with indoor arenas, heated washrooms, and so on to modest two-stall barns where a professor tends her own aged gelding. This is the horse she has had since girlhood, and this creature biting at my sleeve is the macho Shetland pony who serves as his stable companion.

I am told many an equine tale. The editor of a midsize daily newspaper who teaches journalism at the Atlantic-coast college where I'm to read explains how she put herself through college as an exercise girl at the local racetrack. Her first time out, two jockeys rode up along either side of her horse and carried her off at a flat gallop.

She had never galloped a thoroughbred racehorse before and was so terrified that she wet her pants. Enraged and humiliated in equal measure, she fought back tears as she slid off the horse, meanwhile trying to hide her wet britches. "It was the ordeal," she said, "right out of the Middle Ages."

From that moment on, though, the jockeys were wonderfully chivalrous. They cantered around the oval with her decorously, helped her saddle fractious horses, gave her a leg up, and made her life at the track quite livable.

She tells me this over complimentary dinner, the department picking up the check, starved junior faculty members pigging out on roast beef and chocolate mousse, the poet content with a salad and a roll. After the reading and book signing, several of us gather for coffee and brownies. It gradually becomes clear that there is something they want me to know.

I hear about Anne Sexton's reading at this very institution in the last year of her life.

Of course they all went out drinking afterward. Anne had them read her poems aloud to her, every poem from the reading she had just given, and many from earlier books. It was a memorable roistering evening. I think to myself how glad I am to be too old to go out drinking afterward and roister. Farewell, old roistering days! Farewell, too, old best friend Anne, trying so hard to stay alive that she had to have casual acquaintances read her poems back to her to make sure she was still sentient.

I have mourned Anne, we have all mourned Anne, and she has taken her place in the canon. But somehow I am sadder for Cathy, whom I failed to comfort, who is very likely still alive and may or may not be writhing her way to madness and death.

TRANSLATIONS

William Cliff is the pseudonym of a Belgian poet who writes in French. His first book, *Homo Sum,* published by Gallimard in 1970, was read in manuscript by Raymond Queneau, the well-known novelist and poet, whose *Zazie dans le métro* was made into a very successful film. In an introduction to the second edition of *Homo Sum,* written by Claude Roy after Queneau's death, Roy reports that Queneau found Cliff absolutely without equal. He called attention to his delectable moroseness, a person with three strikes against him: born in the Brabant region, *émpetré*— literally, hobbled—by his origins; homosexual; and of no faith in himself or in a supernatural being. Roy calls him a Leopardi of the pavement, a badly raised Ecclesiast, and goes on to set the stage for Cliff's main theme: an evening of masturbating in the corner by a sad fire, amid the powerful scent of a young woman. He is a garçon in blue jeans waiting for the bus and assailed by the ludicrous nothingness of existence as he stands without any social clothing or manners between him and the outside world.

My daughter Judith was a simultaneous interpreter for the European Common Market (now the European Union) in the seventies. Married to a Belgian, she was conversant with the subtle differences between French French and Belgian French—they are considerable. Neither of us can remember how we came to meet Cliff, or he to meet us, but there he was—I think somehow he came to call—unassuming, sweet, a humble poet whose birth

79

name is André Imberechts, clearly a Flemish name, though he spoke and composed in French. In conversation he used his birth name. William Cliff, he confessed, was the name of his first lover, a Canadian. We met a few times while I was visiting, and then Judith and I began to translate some of his appealing poems. I couldn't get Judith to tackle any of the Masturbation series, Roman numerals I through V, or the poem titled "Coitus" or the one called "Fellatio"—they were too graphic for her conservative tastes—but we agreed on several others. We also translated several francophone women: Denise Jallais, Anne Hébert, and others. But then Judith left in midproject to take a UN job and soon departed Brussels for Bangkok. This year—she is now stationed in Ottowa, Canada, and drives down frequently—we tried to reconstruct our foray into Cliff, and just on a whim we googled him. To our delight, there were lots of hits. We also discovered that Gallimard had reprinted his first two books, *Homo Sum* and *Marcher au Charbon,* in a single edition. (Parenthetically, I invite anyone to come up with a reasonable equivalent for the latter title.) Cliff has also written his autobiography in prose but there is no mention of it online and I cannot find my inscribed copy of it.

The two following poems are going to seem very simplistic, without nuance, and not really representative. André wrote many poems about his childhood—he was born just after World War II into a culture of shortages, unemployment, and the despair of wounded and maimed returnees. He wrote fiercely ironic poems about these subjects, about his sexual exploits, and about the factionalism that still mars Belgium: Flemish, that is, Dutch-speaking, against French-speaking; agrarian culture against urban. We chose these poems because they seemed the most accessible.

HESBAYE [A FERTILE PLATEAU IN THE BRABANT REGION]

Reclus aux mornes murs ou par un dur hiver j'ai vu
mon premier jour, souvent je grimpe sur la bicyclette
qui toute à rouille et cris m'emporte aux champs
        parcourus
de machines. C'est la moisson. Et tant pis pour mes fesses;
le pavé belge pourra bien te durcir, mon pauvre cul,
mais il faut que je m'en aille de ces maisons muettes.
Bon. Nous sommes dans l'énorme campagne
        brabançonne.
Interrogeons ce ciel, ces champs, ces carrés de moissons,
ces maigres arbres parfois oubliés entre deux bornes,
ces chemins dessinés par le travail et les saisons.
Je veux interroger un pays où ma soif réclame
des héros, un art, oui, quelque fierté d'être le fils
de ces sillons, de ce limon riche et lourd et qui bave
par flots tout ce froment noirâtre sali par la pluie.
Je voudrais que jaillisse aux profondeurs de ce ciel gris
de quoi réveiller mon coeur écoeuré, une vraie rage
de rire, de jeter la joie à tous les vents, un cri,
l'epouvante d'une armée d'oiseaux, un gamin surpris . . .
Et déçu je circule sans égard pour la douleur
de mes deux fesses sur ce vélo tout à rouille et cris;
se plongeant avec amour dans la boue le chien me suit
comme il peut et je plisse les yeux et j'ai peur j'ai peur:
le ciel, les champs, le chien, les gens, tout est normal ici.

Here's our rendition. We didn't attempt to reproduce Cliff's rhyme scheme.

Monklike behind the same gloomy walls where one hard
    winter
I first saw the light of day, often I climb on my bike
that's all rusty and squeaky but takes me to the fields
    that are
crawling with big machines. It's harvest time. And tough
    luck for my buttocks;
the Belgian cobblestones will harden you up, poor old ass,
but right now I've got to get away from these silent
    houses.
Good. We're in the enormous Brabant countryside.
Let's examine this sky, these fields, these squares of
    waiting grain,
these skinny trees sometimes forgotten between two
    boundaries,
these paths laid out by labor and seasons.
I want to examine a landscape where I hunger for some
real heroes, for art, yes, some pride in being the son
of these furrows, of this rich and heavy alluvium
that disgorges all this blackish wheat dirtied by rain.
I would like something to spurt from the depths of this
    gray sky,
something to rouse my disheartened heart, a true frenzy
to laugh, to hurl joy to all the winds, an outcry,
scaring an army of birds, a surprised street kid . . .
And disappointed I pedal on without regard for the pain
this rusty squeaky bike inflicts on my two buttocks;
plunging with love into the mud, a dog follows me
as best he can and I screw up my eyes and I'm full of
    fear, fear;
sky, fields, dog, people, everything's normal here.

And the second poem, from *Écrasez-le,* published in 1976, a slightly disguised sonnet, in which we did attempt to reproduce the rhyme scheme:

ÂGE ADULTE

Oh! que c'est fatigant de figurer dans un salon
de languir et mourir en tricotant conversation
alors que du soleil taille des trous dans les nuages
et que le vent puissant secoue les toits sur nos ménages!

J'ai pris congé des snobs des cultivés des littéraires
pour foncer dans les gens courant à leurs affaires.
J'ai faim d'espace oh! j'ai faim d'un dieu jeune et
    caillouteux
comme un chemin de France libre entre ses arbres hirsutes
où l'on sent au détour des habitants et des cahutes
la force innée du monde et des tombes et des dieux.

Mais voyant dans la ville un gosse en short sur son vélo
je me dis qu'il est trop tard pour rêver du miracle
qu'à mon âge il vaut mieux me trémousser dans les
    cénacles
et prendre pour vraie vie leurs plaisanteries et trémolos.

ADULTHOOD

Oh how tiresome to be part of a literary salon
to languish and die knitting conversation
while the sun sculpts holes in the clouds
and the stout wind rattles the roofs of our households!

I've left behind the snobs, the cultured world of the arts
to plunge into people who play their own parts.
I'm starved for space, oh! starved for a young god as stony
as a road in France coursing between unpollarded trees
where on the curves you can sense the people and their
    shanties,
the innate force of the world and its tombs and deities.

But seeing a kid in shorts downtown pedaling
tells me that it's too late to dream of miracles,
that at my age I'm better off fluttering about in cenacles
and taking their witticisms and tremolos for the real thing.

AUDIENCE

As Jarrell said, the days when people stood on chairs to catch a glimpse of Alfred, Lord Tennyson, are gone, along with the snows of yesteryear. Poems, in those good old days of Palgrave's 1861 edition of his *Golden Treasury of the Best Songs and Lyrical Poems in the English Language,* provided a commonality of experience in every literate household. "Hail to thee, blithe spirit" and "Let me not to the marriage of true minds" were easily accessible to a generation that had psalms and hymns by heart as well. In a not-yet heterogeneous, multicultural population, the Bible and Shakespeare, along with Donne and Herbert, Keats and Shelley, served as foundation stones for the education of the young.

In a preliterate society, the poet was shaman, mythmaker, historian. The tribe survived because the life of the individual was subordinate to the needs of the majority, and the poet communicated the tribe's values through storytelling. Some sort of rhyme scheme and refrain was a way of remembering myth and metaphor. Long before the troubadours of the Middle Ages rode from village to village, the lives and loves of the gods were handed down, mouth to mouth, from generation to generation.

In an essay on the ghazal, a Persian/Arabic form written in strongly end-stopped couplets, the Kashmirian poet Agha Shahid Ali describes this gala event: "At a *mushaira*—the traditional poetry gathering to which sometimes thousands of people come to hear the most cherished poets of the country—when the poet recites the first line of a couplet, the audience recites it back to him, and then the poet repeats it, and the audience again follows suit."

At the dedication of a new hydroelectric station in Siberia, as many as forty thousand people are said to have assembled to hear the Russian poet Yevgeny Yevtushenko recite his "Bratsk Station" in praise of its construction, an act that also helped restore him to political favor. In Latin America, a poet can also be a statesman or a governor or senator and command large public attention, as did Pablo Neruda.

In our own country, Jimmy Carter, a lifetime reader of poems, aspired to be a poet himself and sought instruction in poetry from established contemporary poets. In 1980, he and his wife hosted an extraordinary gala for poets, inviting almost a hundred to attend and twenty of this number to give brief readings. As one of the poets invited to read, I have vivid but staccato-like impressions of the event. Philip Levine, Sterling Brown, and I read for ten minutes apiece in what I have ever since referred to as the Rutherford B. Hayes room. There, in a capacious china cabinet, is enshrined a trapezoidal turkey platter of substantial proportions used by President Hayes for serving the Thanksgiving turkey.

In 1998, Robert Pinsky, the poet laureate, a new designation for the post that was formerly called consultant in poetry to the Library of Congress, hosted another gathering at the White House, where selected poets were invited to read from the works of earlier bards. Pinsky deserves credit also for innovating the Favorite Poem Project, assisted by Maggie Dietz. Launched on Valentine's Day—a traditional day often marked with verse, sometimes mere doggerel—the project invited people to submit their favorite poems to an international Web site, www.favorite poem.org. In the opening year, eighteen thousand responses were collected, from kindergartners to the elderly, drawn from every state, and representing widely diverse backgrounds, occupations, and levels of education. These entries were winnowed down to a workable number and recorded, along with the individuals' statements—often artless and charming—about the poems they had written. In addition to anthology texts, fifty short video documentaries were culled from these entries, and ongoing readings and summer poetry institutes continue to thrive. The huge success of this project is heartening.

Pinsky has made a very telling and poignant point with his project. Not only has it proven that the affectionate audience for poetry in this country is broad and lively, ranging from pipe fitters to sheepherders, schoolchildren to bankers to trapeze artists, but, as he is quoted as saying, "Imagine if we had an archive of this kind from the year 1900, or the year 1800" (Maggie Dietz's article on Robert Pinsky's Favorite Poem Project, *American Poet* [Academy of American Poets bulletin], Spring 1999). It would have been an enormous cultural resource providing insight into what Americans thought and felt. Now, posterity will have this archive from the millennium. Moreover, the project reinforces my personal passion for having poems by heart, providing, as it were, the very best imaginable audience of one.

This same affectionate audience is evident in Russia as well. In 1999, that nation celebrated the 200th anniversary of the birth of Alexander Pushkin. Although Pushkin, who died in a duel at the age of thirty-seven, is Russia's most celebrated bard, the degree of poetic frenzy this bicentenary evoked had not been anticipated. Pushkin's visage appeared on posters and billboards, T-shirts and candy wrappers. Thanks to the enterprise of Yevgeny Gorelets, a freelance television producer, his best-known verses were recited daily by ordinary Russians who were filmed as they faced the camera. "Eugene Onegin," a romantic narrative poem of 389 stanzas, most of them fourteen lines in length, was declaimed by "bakery workers, homeless people, politicians, actors, outlaw bikers, pedestrians, farmers, coal miners, hikers, prison inmates, students at an institute for the blind—all sharing a common love for Pushkin," according to an Associated Press dispatch by Mitchell Landsberg.

Sit-down audiences in auditoriums or libraries, bookstores or community centers, drawn in as for a play or sporting event, pay homage to poetry as an art form. Occasional poetry—poetry glimpsed in subways or buses, poetry over the telephone for a nominal charge—may have an even larger though more casual audience. For poetry functions through multiple avenues; not only does the poem have primacy on the page, it is also an oral, aural, and visual experience. To be present when a great poet reads a great poem is surely an epiphany, but there are many stations to visit along the way.

When I was an undergraduate in Cambridge, Massachusetts, in the late forties, public readings were still something of a novelty. The close of World War II thrust some remarkable soldier-poets upon the stage: Richard Eberhart, Randall Jarrell, Howard Nemerov, Philip Booth, James Dickey, William Meredith, Karl Shapiro. By the fifties, readings at colleges and universities not only became an accepted and ever more prevalent art form but also were often subsumed into the contemporary literature curriculum. Honoraria for these readings, usually in the $250–$500 range, typically came out of English departments' discretionary funds plus contributions from small endowments, alumni and alumnae associations, literary magazines, even local businesses. The dinner-before-the-reading, usually prepaid, with appropriate beverages, at the best local restaurant, in time became something of a tradition that persists to this day. Members of the English department, the comparative literature department, even the philosophy department, the provost, the vice-president, and a few hand-picked graduate assistants often took part. Frequently the nervous poet picked away at a spinach salad while the rest of the table attacked the sirloin steak special.

Today, videotapes of historic and contemporary readings have become commonplace. While these usefully supplement class assignments, nothing takes the place of a live appearance. Just as a play on television can only partially capture its essence, so a legitimate theater production, like a live reading, projects the drama to its highest realm.

I had the good fortune to attend readings by some poets who are now firmly fixed in the canon of American letters. On more than one occasion, Robert Frost read to an overflow crowd in Sever Hall, one of Harvard's largest auditoriums, a scene I have described elsewhere. Years later, at the annual Bread Loaf Writers' Conference, he counseled us young poets on the staff to follow his example.

I also heard Auden in that same room at Harvard, and again at Boston College, facing that same rapt audience of hundreds who would live to tell their children and their grandchildren how wrinkled the poet's face was, how casually he was attired—it was his habit to wear bedroom slippers in place of shoes—how brittle and British his tone. Another famous British poet said of him in his last years, "Poor old Auden. Pretty soon we'll have to take off his face and iron it out to see who he is." And while he still read his famous "September 1, 1939" to attentive audiences, his text open on their knees ("I sit in one of the dives / On Fifty-second Street / Uncertain and afraid / As the clever hopes expire / Of a low dishonest decade. . . ."), he dropped the penultimate stanza of this major poem. No longer would he intone the famous lines that ended: ". . . no one exists alone; / Hunger allows no choice / To the citizen or the police; / We must love one another or die." Disillusion had overtaken him.

Some years later, I was privileged to hear John Crowe Ransom read at Tufts University; it was one of his last public appearances. To my surprise, this giant of the Fugitive poets, master of meter, rigorous rhyme, and brilliant metaphor, was physically small. Pink-faced and bald, he rocked back and forth on the balls of his feet as he recited poems from memory. Hearing him say those carefully metered and tightly rhymed poems in his own voice,

Southern to the point of caricature to a Yankee's ear and exquisitely enunciated, enhanced my appreciation of the poem on the page. I never read "Captain Carpenter" now without hearing the Ransom lilt in the final quatrain: "The curse of hell upon the sleek upstart / That got the Captain finally on his back / And took the red red vitals of his heart / And made the kites to whet their beaks clack clack." The satisfaction of those *k* sounds lingers with me, as does the regional term *kites* for buzzards.

Randall Jarrell came to Boston; so did Dylan Thomas. Jarrell sported a frail, see-through beard, but his delivery was robust and his intelligence delighted his listeners. Thomas was sonorous, mellifluous, and, it was rumored, tipsy, though it was hard to sort out alcohol from stage performance. Hearing his villanelle, "Do Not Go Gentle into That Good Night," hearing "Fern Hill" with its dingle, owls, and ricks have fixed these two poems in my memory just as he performed them. The West Coast poet Robert Duncan read turning pages with his left hand as he conducted the orchestra of his words with his right. Batonless, he used his entire arm to indicate stresses and caesuras as he articulated them. Even the white spaces on the page called for his raised hand stilled in midflutter. I was fascinated by his style, much as, years later, I would be caught and beguiled by an Allen Ginsberg recitation of "Howl." Ginsberg, who modeled himself on Walt Whitman, stays in my memory as the most visionary, excoriating, and outrageous performer of our time. Anne Sexton was a close contender for the title of most charismatic confessional poet of the time, rivaling Ginsberg for provocative, even seductive, delivery.

Robert Lowell read with his profile turned to the audience, saying his poems distinctly but in a modest, almost diffident voice. A soupçon of Southern accent, perhaps acquired from the time he spent studying with the Fugitive poets, overlaid his Boston Brahmin pronunciation. Howard Nemerov suffered such severe prereading jitters that we made several circuits of the snowy campus before I was privileged to introduce him to a Tufts

University audience in the early sixties. Once on stage, all traces of nervousness disappeared. He had a way of distancing himself from the content of the poems with witty, offhand commentary; these little verses, he seemed to say, were written by some other person. His listeners were enchanted.

Anne Sexton and I went together to hear Marianne Moore at Wellesley College, although she was all but inaudible, speaking, it seemed, below the microphone and no one daring to interrupt to correct the situation. The tricorn hat was enough. In those days we used to arrive at a reading with the poet's several books in hand. When he—it was almost always a male—announced the title of the next poem, we would rush to the table of contents to locate the poem, then follow faithfully word by sacred word.

I regret that I never heard Elizabeth Bishop or Louise Bogan give a public reading, although I had the good fortune to share a supper in Harvard's Leverett House with Miss Bishop (she showed me pictures of her goats), and John Holmes once took George Starbuck, Anne Sexton, and me to visit Louise Bogan in her cabin at the MacDowell Colony. In "Revisiting the MacDowell Colony," I describe this scene: "We three novices lined up on the lumpy cot / while water was coaxed to boil over the hot / plate and jasmine tea was served in the club / they would never, o never invite us to join. . . ."

Muriel Rukeyser was a poet I admired deeply; in the early days of the Vietnam War, she took a public stance that was courageous and brought down on her head praise and contumely in equal measure. She was the first woman poet I read who was overtly political; this seemed very daring in the tame fifties. However, I only heard her read once, a valiant reading she gave toward the end of her life when she was suffering the aftereffects of a stroke.

My own experience as a poet in the public eye commenced, in a small way, before my first book was published in 1961. Asked to read at a meeting of the New England Poetry Club where I was a new, provisional member, I was catapulted into a state of panic.

Although as an adjunct instructor in English at Tufts University I was teaching freshman composition and American literature to indifferent students, the prospect of reading my own work before a live audience terrified me. It did not console me to be told that many actors suffer extreme stage fright before every performance; that seemed only to validate my own fear.

Now, after forty years of facing audiences as diverse as snow-flakes, I look back with compassion on this person who was racked by such terrible anxiety. Perhaps it is normal, perhaps pathological, to face an audience with a degree of terror that arouses physical symptoms—hyperventilation, shaking, tunnel vision—so severe they almost overcome the speaker. I confess that I took to downing two Bloody Marys in advance of evening readings. There was a thin line between reducing inhibitions to a point where I could function and slurring words so that they were unintelligible and I fear I did not always find it. Partly, I think, I was afraid to succeed in a male-dominated field. Partly, I felt exposed by the emotion of my poems, even the early, heavily Latinate, metrically exact ones such as "Halfway," the title poem of my first book, which opens: "As true as I was born into / my mother's bed in Germantown . . ."

The shorter poems were easier to get through before my voice began to shake. Longer poems that could be counted on to elicit audience response, such as "Fraulein Reads Instructive Rhymes" or "You Are in Bear Country," eased the way, and I came to rely on such poems to launch the program. The bear poem draws on language found in an admonitory pamphlet distributed at the entry points to various parks in the Canadian Rockies. The tone is earnest, the advice full of contradictions. Listeners slowly come to realize that a confrontation with a grizzly may prove fatal no matter what they do: "Courage. Lie still. Sometimes your bear may veer away."

I have never failed to receive appreciative laughter and / or gasps of horror whenever I reach the third stanza of "Fraulein":

"Now look at Conrad, the little thumb sucker / Ach, but his poor Mama cries when she warns him / The tailor will come for his thumbs if he sucks them. / Quick he can cut them off, easy as paper." When did the terror ebb and where did it go? It's hard to say. Somehow, repetition wore down my fear to a manageable nub.

Some venues were more hospitable than others. Reading sitting down, thought by some to be chummy, is something I dislike. It feels unnatural to me to say my poems as if the hearers and I were having a casual conversation. A platform with a podium, an adjustable microphone and light, and a glass of water were usually provided, but there were, inevitably, lapses. At Stephens College in Missouri I remember having to rest my books on a flimsy music stand. Every time I put any weight on this contraption, it slowly sank to the level of my knees. In Boston's Hynes Auditorium, I read my poems against the clatter and sizzle of a cooking school demonstration on the other side of a folding partition. In upstate New York, a fraternity party with a live band was taking place next door; somewhere else, during an afternoon reading, huge mowing machines drew close, receded, and returned while I hurried to fit my words into the spaces between rows. At Boston College, an inebriated priest jumped to his feet and recited one of my poems along with me before he was gently led away. (My son, who had accompanied me, said, "That was God's own drunk, Ma.") For years, a deranged fan in Boston followed me from reading to reading. On one occasion she leapt up and denounced me loudly as an impostor. I avoided readings in Boston for fear of these encounters.

In libraries and bookstores there was often vocal competition from other patrons and customers as they wandered through the building. In massive auditoriums, a small audience could be lost, scattered to the four points of the compass. It was an overwhelming task for the poet to draw them together, into the circle of the poem. A small, stuffy room, filled to overflowing, was always preferable. Once, on a State Department Arts America tour, I was invited to read at the U.S. Embassy in Tel Aviv. An enthusiastic overflow audience reached halfway up the stairs, packed the hall, and disobeyed all the fire laws. It would be hard not to read well under such welcoming circumstances.

In Holland, Michigan, arriving on a delayed flight and whisked from the airport to the reading hosted by Hope College, I found myself on stage in a renovated movie theater. Every seat appeared to have been taken. A student jazz group was warming up the crowd. I was overcome with paranoia; everyone would steal away when the poet rose and approached the podium. I was wrong. It was a memorable evening.

One of my duties at the Library of Congress in 1981 to 1982 when I was consultant in poetry was to draw up the list of poets to appear at the monthly readings. Many notable men had taken the podium over the past several years, but very few women had been invited. I was able to ask several outstanding women to give readings. These included Audre Lorde and Adrienne Rich as well as the valiant Josephine Miles, whose arthritic condition made it impossible for her to stand or indeed even to sit upright; she read at a slant. I wish her work were better known today; she was a remarkable poet.

Does the size of the audience correlate with the success of the reading? Not necessarily. Sometimes the turnout for a poetry reading is small, sometimes surprisingly hearty. It isn't the size of the group that determines the level of response. One wintry day I read to a baker's dozen at a charming small library in rural Vermont and the rapport was palpable. At Bucknell University in Pennsylvania, only a handful of listeners braved a blizzard to hear several of us poets take part in a symposium. Again, the response was ardent though unexpected; we hardy few had reached a state of oneness that had nothing to do with the weather.

Rapport between sayer and hearer occurs or fails to occur, and sometimes it is not possible to know how the "pure, gemlike flame" came to life or simply died away. There's a fine line between pandering to an audience and involving it. It's important to me to serve as poetry-evangelist in neutral or even unfriendly environments. To disarm adolescents is often a challenge. It becomes the poet's mission to reach even the bored, lethargic ones who are marking time at the back of the room. Many of them have been turned off poetry by overzealous or fearful teachers; many more have accepted the TV sitcom stereotype of the poet as fop or fool. In the last four decades I've faced a hundred different high school and prep school classes ranging from compulsory chapel attendance at James Agee's old school, St. Andrews School in Sewanee, Tennessee, to a heterogeneous halter- and shorts-clad student body in Coral Gables, Florida. In every group there are a few who thrill to the poems, raise their hands to ask pertinent, even personal, questions. In many cases, students will come up afterward to confess they've never heard a poet read her poems aloud before this, that they were astonished to be able to hear and understand the poems, that until now they had "hated" poetry because they couldn't make sense of it.

What had I done? Nothing remarkable; I had torn down some icons. I talked about the genesis of some of my own poems, discussed a metaphor, explained an allusion. I had asked that they give every difficult poem three chances, three careful readings. If, after that, the poem failed to work for them, they should feel free to move on. (This advice was heresy to some tradionalist teachers.) I counseled the students to take the poem at face value; read it for pleasure, for the story. In my opinion, every poem should offer the framework of a narrative—not a short story, not a plot complete with denouement, but the outline, the ghost-tale that suggests movement. (Other poets may strongly disagree with my premise, theorizing that language, description, and the emotion conveyed are enough to carry the poem forward.) Then let the other level arrive, enter into the ambiguity of the language, tease out the symbol, the metaphor. The poem requires nothing more than your open mind.

While talking to teenagers can be difficult, I prefer it to signing books for collectors, who arrive at the podium before you can step down. They have first editions of all your books, meticulously encased in plastic. Possibly they've read you, possibly they are only interested in your future market value—they expect to outlive you. There's no polite way to escape their importuning as they unwrap one book at a time. (I almost expect them to request that I wash my hands before I sign.) Meanwhile, the people who have bought one or two books from the table at the back of the room and want you to personalize your signature by writing "For Joan and Mike" must wait. Sometimes, too, the poet is faced with a scrapbook, journal, or diary in which all the visiting poets preceding her have written encomia in praise of the hosts. I always find my predecessors' comments far more laudatory and charming than any I am capable of. Then, too, knowing that the next poet on the roster will have to read what I have written induces in me a powerful writer's block.

What poems to read to what audiences is a judgment call. Of course, the poet wants to seduce the listener, wants to carry him or her along on the journey from poem to poem, but there are bound to be pitfalls. Some in the audience will be moved by a love poem, an elegy, a political poem; an equal number may turn a deaf ear to such subject matter. At Brigham Young University, the poet is requested in advance not to read any poems containing profanity or intimate body parts.

Few among us want simply to entertain or to gratify an audience's preconceived notion of our work. Most of us have no desire to be opaque. We would like to build an audience, not bore it. We want to be heard; we would even like to be loved, but not at the price of talking down to the lowest common denominator. Achieving balance may be desirable. But for some, reading feminist poems, antiwar poems, lamentations and rants, historical

THE ROOTS OF THINGS

narratives in blank verse, intricate triolets, or free-verse gay love poems overshadows all other concerns the poet may have about audience. I feel that the poet is entitled. The poet needs to be himself or herself, come what may.

When I teach poetry seminars I always require my students to attend two or three public poetry readings in the area and write a brief report on one. I am trying to make the point to them that poetry is aural and oral as well as written. They also must read their own poems aloud in workshop, after having asked a fellow member to read first. This gives the poet an opportunity to hear how the poem is perceived and then to apply the proper corrective in his or her own voice. For doesn't every M.F.A. candidate in poetry cherish a secret hope of becoming the public figure invited to stand at the lectern and read his or her own work to a worshipful audience?

In the early seventies Anne Sexton joined forces with a trio of rock musicians to form a group called Anne Sexton and Her Kind. I hated what they did; I felt that the music cannibalized the words and that to rise above it Sexton read ever more melodramatically, doing a grave disservice to the poems themselves. I did not know how popular this blended art form was to become, or how much my cranky ear might over time be trained to appreciate new conjunctions.

Today, music marries poems in a dozen different venues ranging from cafés and bistros to the concert stage and the college auditorium. At a recent Dodge Poetry Festival, before an audience of two thousand, Joy Harjo mingled words with saxophone in a stunning display. Is this blurring of distinctions between genres good for poetry? Well, if it exposes more people to the language of the poem, I reason, it can't be bad. Consider what has been done at the highest level of musical literacy with the poetry of Walt Whitman: Ralph Vaughan Williams's "A Sea Symphony," Frederick Delius's "Sea Drift," William Bolcom's "Whitman Triptych," and, perhaps best known, Paul Hindemith's requiem for Franklin Delano Roosevelt, composed in 1946, titled "When Lilacs Last in the Dooryard Bloom'd." What attracts composers is the melodic quality of Whitman's lines, his dramatic imagery, his essential "American-ness." Once viewed with disdain for his celebration of soldier and prairie, of himself and his homosexuality, Whitman has undergone rehabilitation. Scorned by Ezra Pound and Henry James, once derided as ninth-rate and banal, Whitman is now firmly lodged in the literary canon (Paul J. Horsley, "Transmuting Whitman," *New York Times,* May 16, 1999). For the one hundredth anniversary of his death, more than two thousand people jammed the Cathedral of St. John the Divine in New York City to hear several well-known contemporary poets read Whitman's work aloud.

In an essay originally printed in *Harper's Magazine* in 1989, Donald Hall, one of our canniest poets, who is also an essayist and commentator on the literary scene, debunks the frequently heard charge that poetry is dead. "More than a thousand poetry books appear in this country each year," Hall states, although he is quick to grant that "poetry is not as popular as professional wrestling. More people write poetry in this country—publish it, hear it, and presumably read it—than ever before."

I suspect that Hall's "more than a thousand" books of poems has escalated considerably in the last ten years, thanks to the proliferation of small presses and the new poetry lists undertaken by virtually every university publishing house in the country. Nor is it only the number of books published. Farrar, Straus and Giroux, one of New York's most prestigious publishing houses, sold over a hundred thousand copies of Ted Hughes's *Birthday Letters,* poems about the British poet laureate's doomed marriage to the famous suicided poet, Sylvia Plath, an American (Martin Arnold, "Making Books: A Place For Poets, Perhaps Not For Giants," *New York Times,* January 14, 1999). And Alfred Knopf, another premier publisher, sold a quarter million copies of poetry books, both cloth and paper, in the preceding year, a figure that includes their Everyman's Library Pocket Poets series of thirty titles, featuring such icons as Emily Dickinson (ibid.). The reason for this growth industry? More prizes for first books, more small presses, more M.F.A. programs in poetry encouraging poet wannabes to realize their dreams; more readings in bookstores in malls as well as on university campuses, in community centers, in cafés, even in nursing homes; more public poetry slams with cash prizes for the poet whose poem receives the loudest applause; poems visible to the casual eye on subway and bus placards; poetry in the schools nurtured by young visiting poets underwritten by states' arts councils and the National Endowment for the Arts. The language of poetry was at one time male, middle class, and white; now, it is polyglot, non-gender-specific, multicultural, and not necessarily polite. Rap, for example, breaks more than the rules of grammar.

Poetry slams began at the Nuyorican Poets Cafe in East Greenwich Village, in New York City, in the eighties. As their name suggests, the early "slammers" were New Yorkers of Puerto Rican ancestry. The subject matter was often politically radical. Slam poems today are declaimed at the top of the poet's voice. They depend heavily on almost primitive layers of assonance and alliteration, as did such early English epics as *Beowulf* and *Gawain and the Green Knight.* At the annual National Poetry Slam, up to fifty teams of four poets apiece compete for cash prizes.

Rap poetry or rap music—either term is applicable—has expanded enormously in the last two decades. The poet and critic Dana Gioia sees it as the major new trend of the era (Jesse McKinley, "There's a Resurgence of Poets, and They Know It," *New York Times,* May 30, 1999). He reminds us that rap is written in the same base meter as *Beowulf;* moreover, it is rhymed. The rhymes are not subtle; often they are as banal as the "June/moon/spoon" or "fire/desire" variety. The language is often violent, racist, chauvinist, and sexist. The prevailing rhythm thumps on the ear like bongo drums, perhaps suggesting that modern poetry has traveled full circle from its preliterate origins in chants and songs through centuries of written work to its present oral resurgence. Frankly, I disagree with Gioia. Rap, with its raw bigotry, trite imagery, and dependence on the shock effect of obscenities, can hardly be seen as the new-age poetry of the people, replacing William Carlos Williams or Walt Whitman as the spokespersons for the common man. What rap reflects is social unease, economic disparities, and deficient education. The purpose that it serves is to call attention to these inadequacies. Perhaps, too, it is a safety valve for publicly venting bitterness.

Technology has tapped into a broader audience than could have been imagined fifty years ago. Electronic magazines make poetry accessible to a wide range of potential readers. Many poets have individual Web pages, often established by their fans. Some have blogs in which they discuss their lives, their poems in process, and their politics. Sites such as Poetry Daily and Garrison Keillor's The Writer's Almanac offer a poem every morning to the faithful who sign on. What happens next on the poetry scene is a matter for conjecture.

Whether conveyed in cyberspace, printed on an actual page, or shouted aloud on the street, poetry requires an ardent attentiveness on the part of the audience. There's a kind of contract entered into between poet, the giver, and audience, the receiver, that goes beyond the limited attention span needed to watch a movie or a sitcom. The receiver of a poem has to be an active participant. "A great poem," says Lawrence Raab in an article titled "Poetry's Weakness," "provides many simultaneous pleasures, which are also demands—that we hear, that we think, that we imagine, that we connect" (Lawrence Raab, "Poetry's Weakness," The Writer's Chronicle 31, no. 6). Unlike other art forms in which the listener, visitor, or viewer can either play an active role or simply sit back passively and let the music, dance, drama, or painting wash over him or her, poetry makes demands on its audience. The hearer has to connect with the language. He or she may have a visceral response to its music, to consonance and alliteration, to meter and rhyme, but beyond these not inconsiderable surface delights, the reader and/or listener needs also to experience the surprises of metaphor and symbol, the way familiar words can be wrenched out of their old hiding places into new contexts.

I am not referring here to the language of Shakespeare's time, nor to the metaphysical love poems of George Herbert or John Donne, or even to the lush greenery of Dylan Thomas or Gerard Manley Hopkins, but to poems written in the colloquial speech rhythms of contemporary America. Not, as Marianne Moore wrote, "in Spanish, not in Greek, not in Latin, not in shorthand, / but in plain American which cats and dogs can read!" Perhaps poets in general are defensive about their audiences. Yes, we want them to comprehend a language cats and dogs can read, a language, we pride ourselves, that we are writing in, but it would be gratifying if they also understood our allusions in Latin or shorthand, if their ear and eye were trained to pick up rhythmic patterns, even rhyme schemes. A student fan once came up to me after a reading, full of enthusiastic praise for my poem "Woodchucks." "And the best thing about it," he concluded, "is that you didn't force it into rhyme." The poem, in five stanzas of six lines each, is tightly rhymed *abcacb*— "right / Exchange / bone / airtight / stone / range"—however, I was not offended. A more sophisticated listener might have heard the recurring sounds. Rhyme, I feel, ought to occur subtly and naturally, in cat and dog, so to speak.

What audience are we writing for? Who do we hope is listening to and reading us? The poet in prison, the academic in his or her office overlooking the college quad, the CEO, the assembly-line worker, the lover, the house husband, the mother . . . there are as many answers as poets. Sentenced to death in 1586 by Queen Elizabeth and disemboweled alive before hanging, twenty-eight-year-old Chidiock Tichborne wrote his own elegy, "written in his own hand in the Tower before his execution," almost exclusively in monosyllables ("My prime of youth is but a frost of cares"). It is hard to imagine the poise and strength of character that enabled this young man to compose three six-line stanzas rhyming *ababcc* in perfect iambic pentameter before his execution, each stanza concluding "And now I live, and now my life is done." It is not only a cry from the heart; he is addressing posterity.

Four centuries later, Nâzim Hikmet, in "Some Advice to Those Who Will Serve Time in Prison," counsels ". . . it's your solemn duty / to live one more day / to spite the enemy." Here, the audience is quite simply those who survived the same ordeal or managed to avoid arrest in a police sweep. We cannot help but be moved by the work of so many political dissidents in Eastern Europe and now, increasingly, by oppressed minorities around the world. Poems by Chinese dissidents, for instance, have even given rise to a school known as the poetry of ambiguity, in which metaphor conveys the politics of opposition to the regime.

At the other extreme lie the poems of those who say they write only for themselves. They don't have an audience, they don't desire one. They are not professionals. They do not, for the most part, read the poetry of others. They write out of an inner need to express the intensity of their feelings. Somehow, this position has a disingenuous cast to it. Many of these "amateurs" who ask nothing of an audience do not confine their poems to diaries or journals. Some go on to publish their work privately, paying for five hundred copies from a vanity press to distribute to their friends and relatives and, not infrequently, to published poets and critics as well.

As Lawrence Raab points out in "Poetry's Weakness," one rarely hears a musician say, "I compose string quartets, but only for myself." The diary poem, he writes, is "in the service only of its creator, desiring no other reader . . . since the feverish moment of its composition may have been all that was necessary." Revision, for this writer, may be a violation of the feelings that prompted the poem. "If this is, in fact, the way many people who write but do not seriously read poetry view poetry," poetry is reduced to "a private confessional activity . . . a curious kind of emotional self-indulgence." Such views distance poetry farther from its potential audience, giving it an aura of pretentiousness and exclusivity.

In fact, the poem, like the string quartet, presupposes an audience. The story is not a story until it is told. Some poets may conceptualize the perfect audience of one; others may fantasize for themselves that crowd of forty thousand glistening in the summer sun of Siberia. Still others may have in mind a parent, a teacher, colleagues, both friendly and un-, a lover, a faceless murmuring group assembled in the local library.

Many of us turn away from this question, generally one of the top ten asked in an interview. My own answer is as equivocal as any. I write, first of all, to please myself, although "please" is not an adequate descriptive. Although aware of an audience, desiring a sympathetic, intelligent audience, like the diary-poet, I write for self-gratification. The poem needs to be shaped. It has to meet my own standard for it before it can meet anyone else's, but I want it to be read, listened to, chewed on. In a sense, the poem is not finished for me until it has found an audience. Once in print, it acquires a certain authenticity it lacked while it was still in draft form. Once I have read it to a live audience, it acquires even more modeling. The breath rhythms become more apparent. There are caesuras (natural breath rhythm breaks within the line, indicated here with ||) that I may have been subliminally aware of while I was writing but which now assume a more deliberate stance, becoming platforms, inviting the reader to pause, look back, before going on ("They are weighing the babies again || on color television. / They are hanging these small bags of bones || up in canvas slings").

If the poem is in form, if the rhyme scheme was hard-won, as is usually the case, presenting the poem to a live audience gives me an opportunity to rejoice in the gift of rhyme achieved without any wrenching from the natural word order. Ideally, the power of rhyme lies in its seemingly effortless ability to surprise the reader with its aptness, with imagery that presents a new view. I want to slow down, to enunciate modestly but accurately, so that no words are swallowed and lost. ("I hung my bathrobe on two pegs. / I took the lake between my legs" from "Morning Swim.")

If the poem is built on slant rhymes, I want to say them carefully so that the half-rhymes carry their weight ("and the pond's stillness nippled as if / by rain instead is pocked with life"). English is a rhyme-poor language, built around such restrictive Anglo-Saxon monosyllabic nouns as *life, word, fist, tribe. Life,* for example, yields very few direct rhymes other than *knife* and *wife. Strife* hardly fits my criterion of having occurred in normal usage at least once in the last two weeks. The same applies to *rife. Fife* and *fief* are intriguing possibilities but require specific contexts. The minute the poet eases into slant rhyme by eliding the vowel sound, a thousand permutations for *life* suggest themselves: *grief, loaf, safe, aloof, riff, scoff,* and so on.

These are technical matters. So, too, is the question of the poem's length. It is hard for an audience to follow a long poem, particularly a philosophical one, without narrative guidelines. Without the text in front of them, listeners' attentions stray; a line, an allusion is lost; bewilderment sets in. Sensing this, the reader feels abandoned, grows anxious, wants desperately to put an end to the disaster. I try to avoid presenting in public poems that run over two pages.

Instinct tells me that shorter lyrical poems are better suited for reading aloud to a general audience. Shorter poems give the reader more latitude, allowing the poet to display a broader range of topics: love poems; elegies; political, ideational poems that border on polemic; pastoral and antipastoral poems; cityscape poems; poems about family constellations; and so on.

Building an audience in today's market, so to speak, depends to a large extent on where the poet is, geographically and chrono-logically, as well as on the poet's status in the literary community.

THE ROOTS OF THINGS

The time-honored route by way of publication first in small literary magazines, then in larger ones with a larger audience, then a chapbook or first book, traditionally leads to acquiring an audience, first on the page and, gradually, on the reading circuit. Geographically, the poet who wants a live audience will fare better in an academic setting, where readings are established routes on campus or in the nearby city. Chronologically, it helps to be either young and newly discovered, or old enough to have outlasted many of your peers. (I visualize the university committee sitting around the table, saying, "Let's get Maxine Kumin this year while she's still around.") In the interest of ethnic diversity, more minority poets are being invited to take the podium.

In my lifetime, I have had the distinct pleasure of seeing the audience for poetry by women grow from a tiny, secret cell of listeners to, in some cases, overflow crowds. In the fifties and sixties, women writers were harshly criticized by male reviewers for overtly confessional poems. James Dickey, for example, attacked Anne Sexton's focus on such then-taboo subjects as menstruation, abortion, and menopause; Adrienne Rich regularly drew fire from critics who were offended by her lesbian stance. Carolyn Forché, whose photograph appeared on the cover of *The Country Between Us,* her stirring book of poems about the revolution in El Salvador, was attacked, presumably for going where no woman poet before her had gone, and for allowing her face to appear on the jacket (in my experience, the poet seldom is consulted about what picture is to appear where). This was the price she paid for being pretty.

Recently, in a not untypical interview for a college paper, the reporter set the tone immediately by volunteering, "I have one of your books, *Nurture,* but I haven't read it." His first question was: "Would you say you write academic poems or metaphysical ones?" Taken aback, I asked him to define these terms. "I don't know what they mean," he said. "One of my professors suggested that question."

Next came the three McQuestions of student interviewers: Who is my favorite poet? Which poets have influenced my writing? Which of my poems is my favorite? As usual, I equivocate, naming five or six favorite poets and several more, including the psalmists, who have influenced my writing. My favorite poem, I tell him, is the one I'm working on at the moment.

He understands that I am a nature poet. And that women in general write nature poems. I mention Robert Frost, W. S. Merwin, Gary Snyder, Wendell Berry. Frost is the only one he has heard of. In closing, he says he will "probably" come to the reading. They take attendance and he could use the extra credit.

Not all student interviewers are as crass as this young man. But if the poet sallies forth on the reading circuit, this awaits him or her somewhere on the agenda. Somewhere, too, lurks the night on tissue-paper sheets in the only motel in town, the only window overlooking a bleak barrack of storage sheds, the dawn traffic rife with (there's that rarely used rhyme word) bawling hogs being hauled to the abattoir. On the room's TV, a sitcom featuring an effete character who is of course a poet. Welcome! You are a poet in the millennium in America.

But in all fairness, this scene is counterbalanced by some profoundly rewarding ones. Flowers, fruit and nuts, wine and cheese, even champagne ordered by the women's studies program or an independent reading group await you in Days Inns or Marriotts or in modestly elegant surroundings, sometimes a suite of rooms, in Seattle or Chicago. Or, in the unavoidable instance when you are accommodated in the university guest room or the vice-president's house, a junior member of the faculty takes you home for a breakfast of Irish oatmeal the next morning. Two students meet your puddle-jumper plane in Minnesota or Oklahoma and convey you to a lookout tower to watch the sunset. The forest ranger is a Ph.D. candidate in biology and has all of your books. A poetry workshop you agree to sit in on is alive with exciting work. And, if you have attained my advanced age,

106   THE ROOTS OF THINGS

former students step forward frequently in Newark or Newport, Boise or Buffalo, to tell you how much they enjoyed your class, how important you were to them in making some major career decision, how, heaven forfend! they have named their first child after you. Welcome! This too is poetry in the millennium.

LETTER TO A YOUNG WRITER

Dear Eager One:

As you are now, so once was I, for starters. And I, too, devoured Rilke's *Letters to a Young Poet,* so hungry for scraps of encouragement and solace that I committed whole paragraphs to memory. I still carry around with me "works of art are of an infinite loneliness and with nothing so little to be reached as with criticism" and "await with deep humility and patience the birth-hour of a new clarity." *Letters* is a kind of breviary to be borne in your backpack and taken out from time to time when the hopelessness of it all assails you.

What do I mean by hopelessness? The inability of the poet ever to express to his or her satisfaction what is taking place on the worksheet. The finished poem is found wanting by its creator; it never quite fulfills the writer's expectation, even though it goes out in the world, perhaps gets chosen for inclusion in an important anthology, ends up being studied by undergraduates who must then write a paper about it, and so on.

Pay no attention to the siren song of some would-be poets who claim they write only for themselves. Be honest. Does a composer write a sonata only for himself or herself? Is it a sonata truly until it is played? Of course you want your poems to be published, you will move heaven and earth with your multiple submissions to see your work on the sanctioned printed page.

The main thing is to follow your star. While you are working on your own sheaf, keep an open mind. Broaden your framework by reading outside the single constellation of poetry; read fiction, geology, medical dissertations, ancient history. Reread—for surely you have a solid grounding in the poetry of past centuries—Donne and Herbert, Blake and Smart, Hopkins, Yeats, Eliot, Auden. Set yourself the task of memorizing one poem of the masters every week. (I can't help it that there are no women on this list. There will be, in the next hundred years; and in the hundred after that, women will dominate, for they are writing the most interesting poetry at the present time.) Put these into your memory bank in case you are arrested and go to jail; they will sustain you in your miserable cell.

A. E. Housman is easy to learn by rote, as he used lockstep meters, usually iambic trimeter or tetrameter, and full rhymes to express his lovely lonely pessimism and sorrow; he will be good in prison. Yeats will be harder, but worth the struggle. Hopkins will be hardest, with his delicious quirky sprung rhythm, but never mind. Once you internalize a dozen good poems, their rhythm will subtly infiltrate as you scribble furiously over the next failed poem.

Don't throw anything out. Lines that wouldn't fit, images that fell apart, may prove useful later on. Date every page and save it. You may be famous one day. If not, your progeny will pore over your worksheets and treasure the parent they find there.

Now for the hard truth. Rilke, this man we idolize, was so devoted to his work that he sequestered himself from his family for months at a time, refusing to take part in major events lest these interrupt his muse. Let's face it; he was a prime narcissist. It was a woman—Lou Andreas-Salomé—who rescued him from the doldrums; made him change his given name, René, to Rainer; assigned him to a stand-up desk to improve his circulation; even ordered Quaker oatmeal from the United States to be shipped to Paris for his digestive tract.

Actually, oatmeal is not a bad idea. Courting your muse standing up is a useful ploy. I wish you all the luck in the world and I look forward to your first book. *Bon courage! Sois sage.*

Notes on "Pantoum, with Swan"

This poem arose out of an assignment I had given my M.F.A. students in a seminar rather insouciantly titled by the university authorities "Poetics: Form and Theory." Theory was acceptable. Our reading list ranged from snippets of Aristotle's *Poetics* and Longinus's *On the Sublime* to essays by Pound, Williams, Eliot, and Rich. We discussed the postmodern assassination of iambic pentameter, the history of such movements as Dadaism, imagism, the Black Mountain poets, concrete and algorithmic poetry. But demanding poems in ancient forms from new-millennium students is a daunting task. I proposed that we study, memorize, and then write our own sonnets, villanelles, sestinas, ghazals, and pantoums. This suggestion was not met with enthusiasm.

Nor was the pantoum to be our first undertaking. It devolved that several master's-degree candidates were unfamiliar with such prosodic terms as trochee, trimeter, caesura. Scansion for some was a foreign language. Others could not distinguish blank from free verse or differentiate a Shakespearean from a Petrarchan sonnet. While many had song lyrics by heart, there wasn't much else in their poetry memory bank.

I suggested that the best abstract painters began with anatomy classes. Once they had learned to draw from life, they had a wealth of material to abstract from. Something similar would undoubtedly happen to them, I said. I allowed that I would not judge their forays into form harshly; these were mere exercises.

They need never write another formal poem in their lives after completing the semester's requirement.

Malaysian in origin, the pantoum is enjoying a resurgence among contemporary poets, I told them. We looked at some pantoums together, among them Carolyn Kizer's "Parents' Pantoum," Donald Justice's "In the Attic," and John Ashbery's "Pantoum."

We discussed the requirements: any number of quatrains, lines two and four of the first stanza to recur as lines one and three of the succeeding. The poem is to rhyme *abab, bcbc,* and it generally ends by reusing the opening lines in reverse order, but poets today increasingly take liberties with the rhymes, often forgoing them entirely. Sometimes they bend the repeated lines a little, or content themselves with repeating only a phrase, for the sake of preserving meaning. (These statements were reassuring.)

The pantoum as a first formal assignment works quite well. It allows considerable freedom at the outset but imposes the stricture of repetition. Only one of my students attempted to impose rhyme on his poem. Others took some small liberties with the repeated lines. All of them managed to end by putting the serpent's tail in his mouth, i.e., repeating the opening line as the final one, and many of them declared that achieving this wrap-around effect generated real intellectual pleasure. In fact, even the most jaded grad student in the group said that the assignment had been "fun."

I too, wrote a pantoum. And since Yeats's "Leda and the Swan" is one of my old sonnets-by-heart, I decided to write a riposte to the Irish poet's rape scene. What began for me as an exercise poem in which I took considerable liberties—these, too, gave my students courage to proceed—turned into a cry from the heart, a cry from "a classroom so pale / that a mist enshrouded the ancient religions."

Bits of his down under my fingernails
a gob of his spit behind one ear
and a nasty welt where the nib of his beak
bit down as he came. It was our first date.

A gob of his spit behind one ear,
his wings still fanning. I should have known better,
I should have bitten him off on our first date.
And yet for some reason I didn't press charges;

I wiped off the wet. I should have known better.
They gave me the morning-after pill
and shook their heads when I wouldn't press charges.
The yolk that was meant to hatch as Helen

failed to congeal, thanks to the morning-after pill
and dropped harmlessly into the toilet
so that nothing became of the lost yolk, Helen,
Troy, wooden horse, forestalled in one swallow

flushed harmlessly away down the toilet.
The swan had by then stuffed Euripedes, Sophocles
—leaving out Helen, Troy, Agamemnon—
the whole houses of Atreus, the rest of Greek tragedy,

stuffed in my head, every strophe of Sophocles.
His knowledge forced on me, yet Bird kept the power.
What was I to do with ancient Greek history
lodged in my cortex to no avail?

I had his knowledge, I had no power
the year I taught Yeats in a classroom so pale
that a mist enshrouded the ancient religions
and bits of his down flew from under my fingernails.

THE POET ON THE POEM:
CONTEXTS AND CONNECTIONS

As the situation in Israel looks ever more hopeless, someone wryly remarked that the Jews would have been well advised to accept Great Britain's offer a century ago. Most people have forgotten—or never knew—that in 1902 Joseph Chamberlain, British colonial secretary, held out five thousand square miles in the British Protectorate as a national homeland for the Jews in what was then designated Uganda. After fierce debate in 1903, the Zionist Congress agreed to send a group to inspect the land; another year passed before this delegation's negative response came to a full body vote. In 1905, the Congress politely declined the British offer.

This historical sidebar has ended up on the ash heap of memory, along with the Japanese Fugu Plan to resettle thousands of Jews in Manchuria; the Nazi plan to relocate the entire Jewish population of Europe to Madagascar; and the Galveston Movement, organized by American Jews, that brought thousands of European Jews through this port in the early 1900s.

But how did the poem begin? Not rationally, with a marshaling of the facts listed above. Instead, it came on the heels of a villanelle about a failed suicide titled "The Revisionist Dream." At first glance there is no discernible connection between these two poems beyond the titles. How did I make the leap from "Well, she didn't kill herself that afternoon" to "A paradise in Africa"? This puzzle wants, I think, to remain unsolved. But both poems are wishful, both are reaching for a happy ending, the ending denied them. After these two, I was hoping for some more high-flown titles: "Revisionist Carbon-Dating," "Revisionist Sex," "Revisionist Appetite." And knowing how the lyric line jounces against idea in its stubborn, skewed fashion, maybe at least one of these revisions will yet happen.

I hadn't realized how much jounce, as it were, goes into my titles. Through several worksheets the poem "Mulching" was called "Heartbreak," a bathetic abstraction. Then I moved to "Compost," which bore at least the virtue of specific detail. To students who struggle with abstract titles such as "Despair," I offer three concrete approaches: geography ("First Street, Ridgewood"), chronology ("Living Alone, 1989"), and "furniture"—specific detail such as "Waiting to be Rescued." "Mulching" falls in the "furniture" category. Mulching fits the activity described in the poem while leading the reader a bit astray—the use of wet newspaper is, I hope, somewhat unexpected, as is the context. It took me forever to find the right ending, but finding endings is another subject. It frequently leads to the gnashing of teeth. Sometimes serendipity intervenes.

And speaking of serendipity, Howard Nemerov said that every time he finished a poem he was sure that it was his last. But then the cloud lifted and more poems—uninvited, unexpected—came. He described them as arriving like cluster headaches. I go through something similar, something I think most poets suffer—desolate periods when nothing comes, then the gloom lifts to let the beginning of a poem emerge. I gratefully take what is given, the germ that I struggle to bring into fruition. The failed or unfinished or fragmented lines live on in my Bone Pile, along with prized quotations ranging from May Swenson to Dostoyevsky. Before I became computerized, these pages were all jumbled together in a cardboard box from a laundry that washed and ironed men's shirts (I realize I am dating myself). Now they are still a jumble, no easier to sort, but a comfort to page through on a dark day.

REVISIONIST HISTORY: THE BRITISH UGANDA PROGRAM OF 1903

A paradise in Africa?
How generous of the Brits
to offer a new Jerusalem
to the ardent Zionists,
an ample chunk of fertile land
to plow and plant, that the wandering
Jews might wander no more.

Dispatched, the three-man delegation
returned wild-eyed with tales
of lions, leopards, elephants
roaming the yellow veldt at will.
Also a warrior tribe, the Masai,
handsome as statues, whose cattle, given
them by God, are their Torah.

These are the words of Theodore Herzl:
The natives are to be gently persuaded
to move to other lands. The Maccabeans
(delusional Herzl) *will rise again.*
Pretend that it happened. Pretend
the Masai, proud lion hunters,
somehow became willing partners.

First a trickle, then a torrent.
They came with wheelbarrows, seeds, and hoes.
The proud Masai helped gather cow patties,

watched as these Jewish blacksmiths and tailors
devoutly turned them under the soil,
watched as grasslands gave way to gardens
heavy with peas, cabbages, melon.

They didn't exactly intermarry
but the Jews grew browner, the Masai grew paler
until the plateau was all café au lait.
To fatten the cattle the Jews raised alfalfa.
The Tribe of Masai ate eggplants and greens.
They blessed each other's Torahs. Amen.
The wandering Jews wandered no more.

TAKING A STAND:
IF THIS BE TREASON, MAKE THE
MOST OF IT

I am going to take a heretical position regarding essential reading for poets, whether in a graduate program or writing outside the academy. I frankly do not feel that what they need is texts about writing or anthologies of contemporary poetry. My curmudgeonly advice to these rising stars is to read widely in other fields. Of course, I would say this to any well-educated person, but I urge this catholic approach on poets in particular because, in their zeal to achieve that first chapbook, they tend to lose their peripheral vision of the universe just when it is most needed.

Read botany, astronomy, popular physics. Idle through a good dictionary. Read sociobiological studies, such as Sarah Hrdy's *Mother Nature;* read fiction that dissects social mores—here, all of Jane Austen's and Alice Munro's fiction qualifies; investigate comparative religion, atheism, modern medicine, ornithology, American history. Reading omnivorously will sharpen your senses; if you come across accounts of the extinction of the passenger pigeon and the Carolina parakeet, for instance, you will have gone beyond mere birding into issues of industrialization, shrinking habitat, and so on.

To come to terms with the twentieth century, read Susan Sontag, James Baldwin, Joseph Ellis, Mary McCarthy, David

McCullough, Carolyn Heilbrun. Passionate social history not only has a civilizing effect on readers but may also cause them to develop their own passionate convictions. For a refresher course in your roots as poets, go back to John Donne and George Herbert. A powerful poet writes out of staunchly held convictions and no one held them more strongly than the deeply religious poets of their age. (Note: this advice comes to you from a lifelong atheist.)

As an unrepentant old formalist, I recommend paying attention to a good poetry handbook. There are literally dozens available; the most recent and accessible one I've come across is *The Making of the Poem,* edited by Mark Strand and Eavan Boland, but Lewis Turco's *The New Book of Forms,* Miller Williams's *Patterns of Poetry,* and *Strong Measures,* edited by Philip Dacey and David Jauss, are also excellent.

The best abstract painters came of age studying anatomy and painting still lifes; this provided them with rich material to abstract from. For the poet who intends only to write free verse, it is useful if not mandatory to first take instruction in form. Prosody is a dear school; it pains me to see that, like the study of grammar, it is going out of fashion and that graduate students who cannot tell a trochee from a tree limb can nevertheless be accepted into advanced degree programs.

Nothing infuses the poem as deeply with imagery as time out in the world. I always advise students who plan to go on for an M.F.A. in creative writing to take a year off from the university cloister and garner experience on the job. The relentless nine-to-five spent serving food in a cafeteria, wheeling gurneys in a hospital, pounding out dents in an auto-body repair shop, or setting out seedlings in a plant nursery will nurture the new poems in unexpected ways, not necessarily related to the task as hand. Just as hot chili peppers clear the sinuses, the stringencies of the real world tickle the hippocampus. The hope is that the daily grind, the exchanges with colleagues on the job, and the recognition of diversity in the marketplace will lead not to self-consciousness but to heightened awareness. And heightened awareness invites the Muse, She who brings metaphor and symbol to your hand.

In reply to the question about my private canon, let me say disparagingly that my personal reading habits are haplessly eclectic and voracious. I devour whatever crosses my field of sight: books of poems; seed catalogs; novels; memoirs, especially of poets and other writers; literary journals; and op-ed pages. At random on the long counter that serves as my desk are arrayed the current issues of the *Atlantic,* the *New Yorker, Organic Gardening, Smithsonian Magazine, Poetry, Ploughshares,* and the *Georgia Review.* Abutting these, *The American Heritage Book of English Usage* and *The American Heritage Dictionary.* On the nearby shelf, Marianne Moore's *Selected Letters,* Eileen Simpson's *Poets in Their Youth,* Louise Bogan's *Journey Around My Room,* and Thoreau's *Walden* and *The Maine Woods.* In the reading stand cantilevered over my bed, Margaret Drabble's *The Peppered Moth* has just succeeded Rosa Shand's *The Gravity of Sunlight.*

In the past year I have gobbled up so many books of poems that I hesitate to single out particular names. Robin Becker, Carolyn Kizer, Jane Hirshfield, Marilyn Hacker, Enid Shomer, Philip Levine, Mark Doty, Hilda Raz, Sharon Olds, Stanley Kunitz, John Balaban, Carole Simmons Oles, Maurya Simon, Philip Booth, B. H. Fairchild, and Stephen Dunn represent the tip of the iceberg. I don't read language poets because I can't understand them and I am just old-fashioned enough to expect some sort of narrative flow from a poem. I am perfectly willing to stand still for an elusive, difficult poem; I think it is fair to give such a poem three readings with as unprejudiced a mind as I can muster. But when nothing coalesces for me after these efforts, I pass. This may be my loss, but it is also possible that language poetry is merely a fad and will soon pass. Poetry, made of blood and muscle, music and memory, will endure.

ENTRY IN *POET'S BOOKSHELF*

Virgil, *The Aeneid*
Walt Whitman, *Selected Poems,* ed. Harold Bloom
Karl Shapiro, *Selected Poems,* ed. John Updike
Emily Dickinson, *Final Harvest*
Edna St. Vincent Millay, *Collected Sonnets*
May Swenson, *Nature: Poems Old and New*
Louise Bogan, *The Blue Estuaries*
W. H. Auden, *Collected Poems*
William Butler Yeats, *Collected Poems*
A. E. Housman, *A Shropshire Lad*

My "essential" books include the following:

Virgil's *The Aeneid,* in the Robert Fitzgerald translation, which I reread recently, following on the heels of the C. Day Lewis version. Lewis tries to replicate the Latin hexameter line; Fitzgerald chooses iambic pentameter, which falls more naturally on the reader's ear. His postscript provides a wonderful insight into the narrative. (I haven't sampled the Dryden translation but have been told by Donald Hall that it is the best.) Why *The Aeneid*? Because, like a fruitcake, everything is in it: envy; lust; pity; family loyalty; love; uncontrollable rage; prophecy; the inexplicable actions of the gods, which still act upon us in the form of Government; and luck. Also, it is delicious to read.

Now that we have The Library of America series *Walt Whitman: Selected Poems,* edited by Harold Bloom, and *Karl Shapiro: Selected Poems,* edited by John Updike, are both on my list. Karl Jay Shapiro was a huge influence on my early life as a poet. When I was a freshman, he was the first "contemporary" American poet I read. I was fresh from a survey course in English poetry that stopped with Bridges; Shapiro gave me the courage to try to write about the real world I lived in, too. As for Whitman, I am old enough to remember when he was shunted aside as wild, egotistical, and, gasp! a homosexual, therefore not worthy to be read.

On my list also, Emily Dickinson's complete works, titled *Final Harvest,* and Edna St. Vincent Millay's *Collected Sonnets*—in my opinion Millay's are the best Petrarchan sonnets written by an American poet, although Marilyn Hacker is not far behind her. Let me add that when I was enrolled at Radcliffe in the forties, Millay was scorned as sentimental, domestic, and not worthy of comment. She came into the canon about twenty years later so I have lived to feel justified in my admiration for her work. May Swenson's *Nature: Poems Old and New,* Louise Bogan's *The Blue Estuaries,* and the collected poems of Yeats and Auden are also precious to me. Reading Auden I fell in love with form, and from him I began to see how to work in tetrameter. And Swenson, who wrote all those years in the closet, only toward the end of her life coming out as a lesbian, is responsible for some of the best contemporary love poems, encrypted in big-cat imagery for safety's sake. (See "Foreword to *The Complete Love Poems of May Swenson.*")

Finally, a poet little read today: A. E. Housman. I have much of *A Shropshire Lad* by heart, having first encountered it as a lonely adolescent, a time when lugubrious melancholia and dying for love are especially attractive. Five years ago, recuperating very slowly from my 1998 accident, I rememorized these poems from my dog-eared copy, which is small enough to fit in the palm of my hand, like a priest's breviary. I walked a mile slowly, eight times around our driving ring each day, while reciting "Bredon Hill," "Is my team ploughing," the first line of XXVII of *A Shropshire Lad,* and "To an Athlete Dying Young." I think that having poems by heart not only provides you with an internal library to draw on once you are taken political prisoner, as I say to students who cannot imagine caring about anything deeply enough to go to prison for it, but also plants those rhythms next to the heart, where they thrum forever, systoles and diastoles of another life-giving system.

On "Four Poems About Jamaica,"
by William Matthews

I chose Bill Matthews's "Four Poems About Jamaica," from *Rising and Falling* (1979), in part because they are so accessible, so objectively reported by the observer, and at the same time so deeply attached by reason of the white person's sense of guilt and his shame as a mere tourist in a land of poverty and suffering.

The pleasure to be taken from this first poem, "Montego Bay," is to see how skillfully, even offhandedly, Matthews sets his point of view apart from the life he is witnessing. In an interview with Peter Davison of *The Atlantic* conducted just two weeks before his sudden death the day after his fifty-fifth birthday, he discusses subject matter. He says, "You don't take on subject matter because of an objective sense that one sort of subject matter is more important than something else. You take on what you can handle, what you can transform, what you can make your own, what you can make explicable and clear to somebody else."

Here, from the outset, looking down, one presumes, from an airplane, Matthews projects the air of an innocent seeing Montego Bay as an artist might: "[a] chandelier, a tiara, / a hive of lights."

I. MONTEGO BAY, 10:00 P.M.

A chandelier, a tiara,
a hive of lights. A cruise ship

is leaving, the S.S. Jesus
again, the only ship that comes

here. If I watch the ship go
long enough I become the ship.

So rather than leave I look away—
because the sea is a foreign country

and I love to travel, but not
like a faltering heart

set on fire and pushed out to sea
not like a birthday cake.

In the next poem, "Jamaicans Posing to Be Photographed," he
makes clear the disparities between himself—literate, educated,
and in possession of a camera—and "illiterate Esther," who asks
him, "Can you hear from the dead / with that box?" Others pose
in "full dress . . . as if . . . these were wedding / pictures, since white
folks care // about weddings." This poem is twenty-five years old;
one doubts that the Jamaicans are still naive or superstitious, but
perhaps if they don't care about weddings it's because they simply
can't afford to.

Illiterate Esther watched me
closing a book and asked,
*Can you hear from the dead
with that box?* God yes.

Today I take pictures.
My subjects are full dress.
My subjects! As the language
I live by flows through me

it carries so much history
I'm embarrassed, I who believe
in language and distrust
its exact parlor tricks.

Full dress, historical
posture, as if they were running
for office or these were wedding
pictures, since white folks care

about weddings. Somber Ronald,
age three. And Esther, archival,
though the dead don't live in boxes
and nothing keeps in the heat.

Matthews's declarative tone sharpens in the third poem, "A Hairpin Turn Above Reading, Jamaica": "Only // the rich live this high, with a view / of the bay, and the rich / will be with us forever, . . . The rich buy truckloads / of water and hire the poor / to drive them up. Water will go / uphill if money will go down." He has shaved the cliché, the poor we have always with us, and made plain the unspoken truth that the wealthy will overcome all obstacles to their comfort. It's of little consequence that "the fire truck fell / beached on its side" and the house it was trying to save up on the heights burns down and "the pump at the base / of the mountain burns out // and the Socialist party, in power, / is sorry." Free of adjectives, this poem is written in the present tense, much as a newspaper reporter might record the scene. In his own words it is "interesting because it is hard to describe and the job of a writer is to describe it." Matthews compares himself and his companions to the buzzards (actually, anhingas) who "perch and spread / their wings to dry, like laundry. / My friends and I are the rich, // though the house is rented."

3. A HAIRPIN TURN ABOVE READING, JAMAICA

(for Russell Banks)

Here's where the fire truck fell
beached on its side, off the road.
So when the fire fell into itself
we came down the hill to watch
the fire truck get saved. Only

the rich live this high, with a view
of the bay, and the rich
will be with us forever,
though the pump at the base
of the mountain burns out

and the Socialist party, in power,
is sorry. The rich buy truckloads
of water and hire the poor
to drive them up. Water will go
uphill if money will go down.

Today there's a goat in the bend,
stolid and demure. She'll move
soon: there's nothing to eat in the road.
A cow and two egrets tack
into the shadow of a mango.

It's noon. Above the bay, turkey
buzzards sift the thermals.
At dawn they perch and spread
their wings to dry, like laundry.
My friends and I are the rich,

though the house is rented. We'll fall
away, the goat will loll off the road,
the bad clutch in the van will slur
but we'll make it up, and we do,
heat-steeped, thoughtful, and sleepy.

Finally, the poet's pronouncement on Kingston, four five-line stanzas that begin with the camera again: "No photograph does justice, etc., / but what does a photograph care / for justice?" With painful detachment, further declarative statements: "Hovels seen from far / enough away they look picturesque" and "Here's / a family of three living in a dead car. / The guidebooks warned us away // from this" and then, his one moment of actual personal involvement surfaces: ". . . and so we came, / ungainly, spreading / our understandings of sorrow like wet wings. / We turn and turn, but everywhere is here, / a blurred circle of wing scuffs."

4. KINGSTON

No photograph does justice, etc.,
but what does a photograph care
for justice? It wants to be clear,
the way an angel need not mean,
but be, duty enough for an angel.

No angels here. Hovels seen from far
enough away they look picturesque.
The blatant blue sky so cool in pictures
is gritty with heat. The long day stings.
We squint at the lens. Though the lines

in our faces are engraved by the acids
of muscle-habits, not by tears.
Sympathy we have to learn. Here's
a family of three living in a dead car.
The guidebooks warned us away

from this, and so we came,
ungainly, spreading
our understandings of sorrow like wet wings.
We turn and turn, but everywhere is here,
a blurred circle of wing scuffs.

These poems were written fairly early in Bill's career. They
appear in his third book but his later work is no more shapely.
One senses that providing a stanza pattern is his one conces-
sion to formalism. The jazz poems, by contrast, have an interior
music. But he made his mark, and I paraphrase his own words,
by paying acute and large attention to the world.

REMEMBERING PETER DAVISON

I've known Peter Davison ever since we became poets, a very long time ago, indeed. But Peter at his best went unrevealed to me until we were stranded together in a blizzard in upstate Pennsylvania about ten years ago. Nor were we alone. Grace Schulman, from New York City, and Ruth Fainlight and Al Alvarez and his wife, from England, completed the entourage. Only a handful of brave souls had struggled through heavy snow to assemble for our readings in commemoration of Sylvia Plath's birthday (or death day, I don't remember which). The following forenoon, a graduate student delivered us all to the nearest airport—we had arrived by several routes, but were to depart en masse for New York, where the program was to be repeated that night at the 92nd Street Y. Apparently, our driver had not checked with the airline, for no sooner had her taillights disappeared in the still-snowy distance than the cancellation of our flight was announced.

Resourceful editor Davison took charge. Because Dr. Alvarez could not be separated from his pipe for the four-hour drive and Grace Schulman could not breathe in the presence of tobacco smoke, he rented two vehicles. The Alvarezes set out in one, Grace, Ruth Fainlight, Peter, and I in the other. As the only licensed drivers, he and I took turns behind the wheel. We stopped for a merry lunch en route and, thanks to his dexterity with the roadmap, arrived in Manhattan unscathed.

I was fortunate to have Peter, as poetry editor of the *Atlantic,* accept several of my poems over the course of his tenure. But we frequently sparred over his suggested revisions. On one occasion he insisted that I drop the last line of a poem; I refused, he refused to relent, and our standoff ended with the poem unpublished. The same problem arose with another proposal: this time, that I delete an entire final stanza. I agreed, then restored the offending lines when the poem, "The Word," was included in my next poetry collection. Sometimes, at readings, I posed this issue to the audience and had them vote on which was the better ending.

Today, all these years later, I wish I could tell Peter that I think he was right.

ON JANE KENYON

Dinner at Jane and Don's. I am unable to pinpoint the date but it must have taken place in the early eighties. All four of us were still relative newcomers to New Hampshire. In 1975, after his grandmother's death at the age of ninety-seven, Don and Jane had come back from Michigan to Eagle Pond Farm. The plan was to spend a year there, but at some point the decision was taken to make this a permanent move. They went back to Ann Arbor to pack up the house and then returned to Don's grandparents' farmhouse for good.

In 1976, the last child gone, we had made the decision to move full-time into the ancient farmhouse we had bought on the cheap in 1963 and used carelessly as a summer camp and weekend retreat for thirteen years. Repairing roofs, dealing with recalcitrant plumbing, and discovering gap-toothed hay rakes and broken bits of workhorse harness in old barns were endeavors we two couples had in common.

Before dinner, a tour of the Hall/Kenyon renovations. The old first-floor bathroom was no more. The bedroom had been reborn as a modern bath and laundry. A new bedroom extended from the back of the house. A sign over the bathroom door announced that this was the Caldecott Room, a nod to the children's book prize Don had won for *Ox-Cart Man* in 1980, which had made these renovations possible. The ell created by the addition allowed for a secret garden, its bricks laid by Jane, where she cultivated her lilies—lilies that "toil not, nor do they spin"—and labor-intensive peonies. It was high summer and I remember the peonies, both burgundy and white, were wide-open. A fulsome and fragrant flower, they had been my mother's favorite, too. No wonder a frisson went through me.

I wish I could say I remember the menu, but I do not. Don's tall, redheaded son Andrew was there, newly graduated from the University of Wisconsin. There were candles and flowers on the table. A good wine went round. Jane served graciously amid the animated conversation. When the main course was completed, she announced that Perkins would clear and bring in dessert. This startled me; I had until then not been aware that someone else lurked in the kitchen, waiting to perform the homely chores of cleaning up. When Don rose and began to gather the plates, I finally caught on.

So much has been said and written about Perkins and Jane that I hesitate here. For more than twenty years we remained friends on our two farms on either side of Kearsarge Mountain, nine miles apart as the crow flies, forty-five minutes by car circling the base. While I may never cultivate a peony, I always think of Jane when our lilies bud up in early summer.

ON KARL JAY SHAPIRO

My freshman year in college, browsing the shelves of the Grolier Poetry Bookshop in Harvard Square, I came upon a new book of poems, opened it at random, and sank down on then-proprietor Gordon Kearney's couch in astonishment. The poem was "University." The book was *Person, Place and Thing,* Karl's first book. "To hurt the Negro and avoid the Jew / Is the curriculum" ran the lines that caused my neck hairs to rise. Five stanzas, unrhymed, all conforming to the pattern of four lines of iambic pentameter followed by three lines of tetrameter, with a concluding dimeter line. A nonce form, adroitly adhered to. The setting, I concluded from the context of the poem, was the University of Virginia, from which one of my older brothers had recently graduated and gone off to war, just as Karl Jay Shapiro had.

Then there was "The Fly": "O hideous little bat, the size of snot / with polyhedral eye and shabby clothes," the daring poet wrote. And a poem titled "Buick," another, "Drug Store." I came to these poems from Robert Bridges and the Augustans. In Robert Hillyer's class we were reading Rupert Brooke. I had no knowledge that modern poetry had opened out to encompass the actual tawdry world we lived in. The tone, the diction, amazed me. Thankfully, I was never the same thereafter.

Then came *V-Letter and Other Poems,* followed by *Essay on Rime,* the latter composed, I've been told, in the field, without reference books to draw on. *Essay* is an overview of form and theory, freehand, as it were. Shapiro's range is exceptional and his insights canny. Even his final note hews to his chosen form:

> The metric of this book is made upon
> The classic English decasyllable
> Adapted to the cadence of prose speech;
> Ten units to the verse by count of eye
> Is the ground rhythm, over which is set
> The rough flux and reflux of conversation.

Shapiro and I met years later, so Sophie, his wife, reminds me, sitting across the table from each other at a literary conference of some sort. But my most vivid recollection is of our rendezvous in an elevator, where, in the few seconds between floors with Karl and Sophie, I managed to blurt out how meaningful his early poems had been to me. Now, rereading his work, I wish we had had more time together, to agree, in the final lines of his *Essay on Rime*, "that / The aftermath of poetry should be love."

CAROL HOUCK SMITH, 1923–2008

Carol was my editor at W. W. Norton over the course of seven books of poetry, one mixed bag of essays and stories, and the memoir of my excruciating inch-by-inch recovery from the carriage-driving accident that nearly took my life. This she extracted from me page by page, barking, "Make it more intimate! Put dialogue in it!"

She was everything an editor should be: compassionate, demanding, supportive, intuitive, and seldom wrong. Over the years she became a dear personal friend. She flew to State College, Pennsylvania, when *Telling the Barn Swallow,* essays by a dozen poets on my poetry, edited by Emily Grosholz, was feted. On the return trip she and my husband Victor explored with gusto their passion for jazz, a topic they never tired of discussing. She came to Boston when I gave the keynote address for the PEN–New England awards at the JFK Presidential Library and Museum. One year at the annual Associated Writing Programs meeting in Chicago we lingered over a private breakfast together.

When we first came together to discuss the formatting of *Looking for Luck,* the initial collection she edited, I happened to be in New York for an event at the Poetry Society of America. They had reserved a room for me at the Gramercy Park Hotel—the old European-style hotel, long before any renovations had even been dreamed of—which barely accommodated a double bed and a bureau. Carol and I laid all the proposed poems out on the bedspread and spent most of the afternoon squeezing around the bed, bumping hips, shuffling the poems about like playing cards before arriving at their disposition into three units. Afterward, we walked several blocks to the art gallery displaying Wolf Kahn's paintings, where we were to select *High Barn & Drop to the Valley* for the book's cover. Carol was quick to intuit my discomfort in the clots of pedestrians thronging around us. "Would you like to hold my hand?" she asked. I did so. Wolf Kahn had been her choice and it proved to be a perfect one. I became his ardent fan; all of my subsequent books bore his paintings on the cover.

But most of all, although to my sorrow she never visited, Carol connected to our farm life. By e-mail and phone we stayed in close touch. I sent her bragging photos of the vegetable garden as the corn shot up to gargantuan heights. Snapshots of the dogs paddling around the pond to inspect frogs and salamanders, and the horses being hand-fed carrots or grazing in sublime pastures ringed with fall foliage. Snow pix, as we dug out from famous blizzards. She was an enthusiastic participant from afar. I find I am still reaching out to tell her, show her, share with her.

LONGFELLOW'S ANTISLAVERY POEMS

In 1842, Longfellow published a little pamphlet of eight poems, all but one of which were written during the last part of his voyage home from Europe that year on *The Great Western*. It was a particularly stormy crossing and while the poet lay sleepless in his cabin for several days, he composed these humanitarian poems on the issue of slavery. Putting aside what one critic called "the abolitionist rhetoric of pathos," it took a certain moral courage to publish them at a time when, to quote Newton Arvin, "anything approaching abolitionism was taboo in respectable quarters, social and literary." It was not seemly for a Harvard professor to reveal his sympathy with the movement, which was regarded as a dangerous brand of romanticism.

Back when he was an undergraduate at Bowdoin, Longfellow had contemplated writing a play about Toussaint L'Ouverture, a freed slave who led a ragtag army in a successful rebellion against Napoleon on the island of Haiti in 1797. The sad fact that the rebel leader was shipped to France in 1802 under suspicion of plotting a further uprising, was confined to an underground cell, was repeatedly interrogated, and died there, supposedly of pneumonia—does any of this sound familiar?—was surely not lost on the young poet, who was known even then for advocating "Negro emancipation."

But the antislavery poems seem to be a direct outgrowth of Longfellow's two-week visit with Dickens in London shortly before he set sail for home. In the course of this time together the two men became staunch friends.

Longfellow read the popular novelist's *American Notes* excoriating the practice of slavery, which Dickens had observed in Richmond, Virginia, during his tour in early 1842. Dickens had come to the New World, he said, to observe this haven for the oppressed only to find an enslaved people in chains. He was particularly appalled by the cruel practice of disfiguring runaway slaves by branding their foreheads once they were recaptured.

From the outset, the Quakers had been abolitionists, but the movement in New England first acquired momentum when William Lloyd Garrison began publishing his newspaper the *Liberator* in 1831. It was not an easy time to oppose slaveholding. Bitter and violent opposition raged throughout the country; Southern slaveholders received the support of Northern merchants who depended on the economics of slavery. Six years later, in 1837, a mob murdered Elijah Lovejoy, a newspaper editor in Illinois, who had published antislavery editorials.

While it is true that abolitionism gradually became an acceptable, even admirable, stance among intellectuals and was endorsed by John Greenleaf Whittier and James Russell Lowell as well as Longfellow's good friend the Massachusetts senator Charles Sumner, it was not, in 1842, a comfortable position to uphold. Whittier's poem "The Christian Slave" was published the following year. It heaps scorn on ministers who endorsed and defended slavery; these ministers became Whittier's favorite target. If anything, this poem is more extreme than Longfellow's. Nevertheless, it earned public attention and acclaim.

Longfellow's little pamphlet struck a chord in Cambridge and was an instant best seller. It elicited a rain of reviews, about half favorable and half condemnatory. In the latter camp, Edgar Allan Poe, writing in the *Aristidean,* April 1845, took on the poet with a vengeance. He not only faulted him for rhyming *abyss* with *witnesses*—"we cannot conceive how any artist could . . . admit such a termination"—and even worse, *angel* with *evangel*—but proceeded to lecture him: this pairing is "inadmissable because identical . . . the ear, instead of being gratified with a variation of a sound—the principle of rhyme—is positively displeased by its bare repetition . . . the rhyming portions of words must always be different."

But the poems themselves he declared "intended for the especial use of those negrophilic old ladies of the north, who form so large a part of Mr. Longfellow's friends." The most controversial of the group is titled "The Good Part, That Shall Not Be Taken Away" and while I promise not to present the seven others in their entirety, I do want to trot this one out for inspection. It's written in the same semiballadic measure as the others.

THE GOOD PART, THAT SHALL NOT BE TAKEN AWAY

She dwells by Great Kenhawa's side,
   In valleys green and cool;
And all her hope and all her pride
   Are in the village school.

Her soul, like the transparent air
   That robes the hills above,
Though not of earth, encircles there
   All things with arms of love.

And thus she walks among her girls
   With praise and mild rebukes;
Subduing e'en rude village churls
   By her angelic looks.

She reads to them at eventide
   Of One who came to save;

To cast the captive's chains aside
And liberate the slave.

And oft the blessèd time foretells
When all men shall be free;
And musical, as silver bells,
Their falling chains shall be.

And following her belovèd Lord,
In decent poverty,
She makes her life one sweet record
And deed of charity.

For she was rich, and gave up all
To break the iron bands
Of those who waited in her hall,
And labored in her lands.

Long since beyond the Southern Sea
Their outbound sails have sped,
While she, in meek humility,
Now earns her daily bread.

It is their prayers, which never cease,
That clothe her with such grace;
Their blessing is the light of peace
That shines upon her face.

Here is Poe again: "The whole poem is in praise of a certain
lady who 'was rich and gave up all' . . . No doubt, it is a very
commendable and very comfortable thing in the Professor to
sit at ease in his library chair and write verses instructing the
southerners how to give up their all with good grace . . . we
have a singular curiosity to know how much of his own, under a

change of circumstances, the Professor himself would be willing to surrender."

It is interesting that the New England Tract Association, reprinting the slavery poems to raise money for the abolitionist cause, found it the better part of wisdom to omit this poem, for few of the rich among them had given up their all.

Perhaps the most influential of the other poems was the one Poe attacked for faulty rhyme (though I note that he seemed not to have noticed the *Lord/record* rhyme in "The Good Part"). Titled "The Witnesses," the poem envisions what lies buried in the ocean as a result of the slave trade: the bones of the drowned, the becalmed, the dead of starvation or thirst, "the skeletons in chains" thrown overboard. These are the witnesses, whose bones "gleam from the abyss," unreconciled to their deaths, watching the world above.

The poem "The Quadroon Girl" evokes the planter who sells his own mixed-blood daughter to the slaver: "Her eyes were large, and full of light, / Her arms and neck were bare; / No garment she wore save a kirtle bright, / And her own long, raven hair. . . . His heart within him was at strife / With such accursèd gains / For he knew whose passions gave her life / Whose blood ran in her veins." Here, the moral corruption of slavery is made eminently clear, though the story is, according to Poe, "the old abolitionist story worn threadbare."

Three poems in this chapbook are written from the omniscient narrator's point of view about the slaves. "The Slave Singing at Midnight" does so "in a voice so sweet and clear / That I could not choose but hear" but, sadly, unlike "Paul and Silas in their prison," no "earthquake's arm of might / Breaks his dungeon-gates at night."

In "The Slave's Dream" the dying slave sees a vision of his native land, quite imaginatively portrayed by a poet living in New England who had never traveled to where "the lordly Niger flowed." The slave revisits his life metaphorically, where "as a king he strode" and sees "once more his dark-eyed queen" and his children. In the final figure of the poem he rides "at furious speed / Along the Niger bank" all the way to the ocean, hearing at night "the lion roar / and the hyena scream / and the river-horse," through forests, across the desert until "Death had illumined the Land of Sleep."

The third, "The Slave in the Dismal Swamp," a horrifying tale of chase by bloodhounds, does not detail the capture but describes "a poor old slave, infirm and lame / Great scars deformed his face," an object so pathetic that one wonders why the slave-holder would bother to try to apprehend him.

It would be nice to think that publishing these stereotyped bathetic poems kick-started the antislavery movement; they were all Longfellow chose to give publicly to the cause. But in February 2007 in Story Chapel at Mt. Auburn Cemetery in Cambridge, Massachusetts, by way of celebrating his 200th birthday, there was a dramatic presentation of Longfellow's connections to the abolitionist movement and the Underground Railroad. He was something of a latecomer; nothing he published after 1842 spoke to the movement, but his account books for the 1850s and '60s show that he actively supported several abolitionist causes, including making donations toward freeing and educating slaves and helping fugitive slaves. In June 1857 he gave money—we don't know how much—"to Mrs. Hillard for Slaves." What's ironic about this contribution is that her husband, George Hillard, was the U.S. commissioner in Boston, responsible for issuing warrants allowing federal marshals to seize runaway slaves after passage of the Fugitive Slave Law in 1850. My source, Michael Kenney, writing in the *Boston Globe,* adds, "he apparently knew of his wife's activities." Kenney also alerts us to a new book by Christoph Irmscher, *Longfellow Redux,* published by the University of Illinois Press. In the introduction, Irmscher states that the book's aim is "to remind us of a poet who pretty much invented poetry as a public idiom in the United States and abroad and who was later shunned by the literary and academic establishment precisely because of it."

I consider the following the most powerful and least clichéd of Longfellow's *Poems of Slavery* because I think it speaks to our present condition vis-à-vis "the vast Temple of our liberties."

THE WARNING

Beware! The Israelite of old, who tore
    The lion in his path,—when, poor and blind,
He saw the blessed light of heaven no more,
    Shorn of his noble strength and forced to grind
In prison, and at last led forth to be
A pander to Philistine revelry,—

Upon the pillars of the temple laid
    His desperate hands, and in its overthrow
Destroyed himself, and with him those who made
    A cruel mockery of his sightless woe;
The poor, blind Slave, the scoff and jest of all,
Expired, and thousands perished in the fall!

There is a poor, blind Samson in this land,
    Shorn of his strength and bound in bonds of steel,
Who may, in some grim revel, raise his hand,
    And shake the pillars of this Commonweal,
Till the vast Temple of our liberties.
A shapeless mass of wreck and rubbish lies.

Introduction to *Perched*
on Nothing's Branch:
Selected Poems by Attila József

White Pine Press deserves a vote of thanks from all of us. In time
for the Frankfurt Book Fair of 1999, which will feature Hungarian
poetry, they have reissued the late Attila József's selected poems,
Perched on Nothing's Branch, in a richly nuanced translation by
Peter Hargitai, himself a native-born Hungarian. First published
by Apalachee Press of Tallahassee, Florida, in 1988, Hargitai's
translation won the coveted Landon Translation Prize from the
Academy of American Poets in 1989 and promptly went into
three editions, a coup for any small press. Now, ten years later,
White Pine is continuing to extend the life of this book.

The trajectory of József's life was a sad one. Ghosted by
frequent nervous breakdowns, hounded by right-wing extremists,
at the mercy of a failed love affair, he took his own life in 1937.
He was thirty-two years old. Here in the West—and perhaps not
only in the West—we have an unfortunate tendency to lionize
our suicided poets, as if to take one's own life confers on the work
left behind a special grace.

Sylvia Plath, like József, was only thirty-two; Hart Crane,
thirty-three; Anne Sexton was forty-five. Berryman was in his
fifties when he leapt, waving, off the bridge; Paul Celan, who
survived eighteen months in forced labor camps only to hurl

himself into the Seine, fifty. In every instance, tormented by their inner demons, it was, nevertheless, the poetry that kept them alive. Plath, after all, had made a serious earlier attempt to kill herself in her adolescence; Sexton, after an initial postpartum depression, had taken a number of overdoses. Berryman had been unable to conquer his alcoholism; Crane, his frequent bouts of depression. Celan never recovered from the horrors he endured under the Nazi regime.

The general public enjoys a kind of prurient interest in these untimely deaths, perhaps taking them as evidence that poets are moral weaklings, effete creatures unlike themselves, unable to stand up to the pressures of daily life. Yes, we would have been richer had Plath, József, and his fellow suicides not succumbed to their separate despairs. The poems they might have written haunt us even today. But let us celebrate what, against enormous odds, they achieved.

We ought also to celebrate poetry itself for sustaining them as long as it did. Certainly for József, poetry provided rich personal rewards, even when he had barely enough money to sustain himself from day to day. All of his poems are cries from the heart, outlets for his supreme though erratic creative drive, his sometimes surreal but surprisingly apt imagery. While *The Columbia Dictionary of Modern European Literature* considers him "the finest Hungarian socialist poet of the twentieth century," to contemporary readers he will seem apolitical, more closely associated with the bittersweet lyricism of David Ignatow or John Balaban.

In a startlingly candid curriculum vitae he composed not long before he threw himself under the wheels of a train, Attila József recounts the dry facts of his life. They make fascinating reading and serve as a window into history as well. Communist, socialist, fascist, schizophrenic—despite the designations society provided, the poems never stopped coming. Happily, the vita is included and any reader of the poems is advised to begin with József's own account of his life. Ten months after composing it, in December 1937, he killed himself. Perhaps it is significant that his adored mother had died at Christmastime. In "Eulogy," one of his most affecting poems, the child's sense of having been willfully abandoned rises to a crescendo of apostrophes:

> I should have eaten you!
> You gave me your own supper—did I ask for it?
> And why did you bend your back to wash clothes?
> So you could straighten it in a wooden box?

Perched on Nothing's Branch contains exactly forty poems, most of them brief, sharp, but invariably built on a scaffolding of arresting images. The poems are ageless, mirroring the human condition and focusing on humankind's existential loneliness. A searing lyric that addresses József's own mental state but speaks in the voice of our own era declares: "I am not the one shouting, it's the earth rumbling" and then proceeds to offer wild strategies for self-preservation: "slink to the bottom of clear creeks . . . hide . . . among insects and stones. / Burrow into fresh bread . . . wash your face in other faces / as tiny blades of grass."

Addressing some of the hazards of translation, Hargitai has said of the first and last lines of this poem that in Hungarian the noun-verb patterns are syntactically parallel, so that literally, the line translates as: "Not I am shouting, the world is rumbling." (Moreover, József's original text of this poem is rendered in capital letters, lest we not hear the intensity of his pitch.) Hargitai explains that Hungarian, like German, has "an agglutinative syntax," which means that prepositions, personal pronouns, and so on get attached to a noun to make a compound word that may require three or even four words in English to achieve an intelligible translation.

Utterly contemporary in tone, many of József's poems ask, as in "Elegy," "Are you also from here? / Where the longing / never ends to be / like another." Often, the diction is flat, deliberately prosaic, then transmutes into a burst of imagery. Soapy water has "a little blue head," "yellow trees stand on one foot" is followed by: "That is all I could write / as I kept falling asleep; / we touched each other." The voice is melancholy and hauntingly modern.

Train imagery appears in several of József's poems. In the lyrical "Autumn," "Weariness squats on a boxcar"; in "Look," "The sun's flaming train / rushes past melancholy doorways." In "Winter Night," winter "streaks into the city / on glittering rails." Even a love poem of loss, "Balatonszárszó," contains a train that has already left. An ambitious poem titled "Consciousness" represents Jozsef's bleak, yet gorgeously defiant, credo. "I have seen / blue, red, yellow in dreams / and felt the order of things—/ not one stone out of kilter," he tells us. He is hungry for certitude: "Living only on bread / . . . / Roast beef does not rub / against my mouth." Despite his searching, "Words lie on one another / like a pile of wood, / squeezing, pressing / each other's being." The last three stanzas of the poem have been hammered on the anvil for precision. It seems that they presage József's final hours.

> A whole man
> has neither mother nor father in his heart.
> He knows that life
> was given in addition to death,
> and he must give it back
> any moment—like the finder his find.
> He is neither God nor priest.

> But I have seen happiness.
> It was soft and blond and 300 lbs;
> its curly smile wobbled in the pen.
> It lay in a warm puddle,
> squinting, snorting. The light
> was tickling its down.

I live near the tracks.
Trains come and go
with glistening windows.
They are the rush of lighted days.
The poet stands in the wisp of compartments,
leans on his elbows and listens.

Only the satisfied pig can be happy, the poem says, suggesting but not stating the Socratic corollary that it is better to be man dissatisfied. It is only a brief leap to the inner landscape of the poet, who observes "the rush of lighted days"—the ordinary, illuminated, orderly life that he is shut out of—from his room overlooking the tracks, while standing "in the wisp of compartments." Translator Hargitai defines these wisps as the fleeting flashes of light that come through the compartment windows as the train flies past. Life, József has already told us, is something he must give back at any moment. At some moment, he made the decision to do so.

Foreword to *Vive o muere,* by Anne Sexton

Well, she didn't kill herself that afternoon.
It was a mild day in October, we sat outside
over sandwiches.

So begins a villanelle titled "The Revisionist Dream" that I wrote about Anne Sexton's suicide, more than thirty years after the actual event. It is the last in a series of poems elegizing that loss, the first written only a few months after she left my house on October 4, 1974, to drive home, close herself in the garage, let the car engine idle, and wait for the death she had pursued—or which had pursued her—throughout the seventeen years of our friendship.

We had met in a poetry workshop in 1957. While we remained advocates of and participants in workshops, we went on to become each other's staunchest defenders and fiercest critics. In the days before computers, e-mails, and texting, we were poets of the typewriter, yellow second sheets, and carbon paper. (My seventeen-year-old grandson asked, "What's carbon paper?") But we were too impatient to exchange worksheets by mail. Because we lived in the same suburb, installing a second phone line was inexpensive. A flat monthly fee permitted us to stay connected for hours at a time when we were working on poems. We whistled into the receiver to call each other to attention.

Suburban mothers of young children, we fought to have our poems taken seriously in the sexist literary culture of the mid-twentieth century. Quaint as it now seems, the women's movement was then in its infancy. As Sexton's biographer, Diane Middlebrook, put it, the prevailing world view of the poet at that time was "the masculine chief of state in charge of dispensing universal world truths." But little by little, our poems made their way up from publication in literary journals with limited readership to the pages of *The Atlantic,* the *New Yorker, Harper's Magazine,* and the *Saturday Review of Literature.*

Tectonic shifts have rocked the intellectual world since those days when women were perceived as capable only of domestic poems, poems about butterflies, spring, and clouds shaped like lambs. From today's vantage point it is easy to see that in the rigid milieu of that era Sexton's poems about menstruation, masturbation, adultery, incest, abortion, and drug addiction aroused furor. Most, though not all, of her critics were male. One wrote that "Menstruation at Forty" "was the straw that broke this camel's back." Another, writing in the *New York Times Book Review,* declared, "It would be hard to find a writer who dwells more insistently on the pathetic and disgusting aspects of bodily experience."

Nevertheless, others, including Joyce Carol Oates and Muriel Rukeyser, found much to their liking. In the critical literature dealing with the body of Sexton's work we can see again and again vitriol and praise arrayed against each other. From this distant outpost, looking back over the highly touted poems of Allen Ginsberg, John Berryman, W. D. Snodgrass, and Robert Lowell, confessional poets all, "the pathetic and disgusting aspects of bodily experience" seem to have morphed into simple, useful material for lyrical narrative, prose poem, surrealism, and slam poetry.

Even before her final collection, *The Awful Rowing Toward God*, Sexton sought to find solace in a father figure. She met with stern disapproval from our original mentor, poet and professor John Holmes, who conducted the workshop at the Boston Center for Adult Education in which we first met. While acknowledging her considerable talent, he detested her subject matter and tried to turn her in a different direction. She was treated by and formed attachments to a series of mental health professionals ranging from psychologists to psychiatrists to psychiatric social workers. One left to establish his practice in a distant city. Another formed a romantic attachment to her and resigned from her case. A third claimed illness and dropped her as a patient, and so on. She was difficult, demanding, needy. Raised as a casual Protestant, she was attracted to what she saw as the salving absolutism offered by Catholicism. More and more her poems featured God the Father and Jesus, whom she humanized in a group of poems known as "The Jesus Papers."

For some years she corresponded with a Jesuit brother. Later, she turned to an elderly priest she had met; at one point she begged him over the telephone to administer the last rites. Certainly he found her distraught and bewildering but he could not meet her expectations. In that bizarre exchange he told her a saving thing: "God is in your typewriter."

Sexton would have reached her eightieth birthday this year, had there been psychotropic drugs available to deflect her post-partum and ongoing cyclical depressions. After several halfhearted and at least two serious attempts to end her life with drugs, she found a way out of her torments at last. Even though I continue to grieve her absence, I feel strongly that poetry kept her alive for those seventeen fertile years and that women poets in particular owe her a debt. In the new country that Sexton colonized, daring to shatter taboos, we move forward, untrammeled by shibboleths or prejudice, poets of our time.

FOREWORD TO *THE COMPLETE LOVE POEMS OF MAY SWENSON*

With rare exception, May Swenson's remarkable love poems, spanning more than five decades, are not gender-specific. Many are cast in Big-Cat roles involving tigers, lions, jaguars, and other shaggy jungle beasts. Others admire or even take the part of circus artists balancing on tightropes.

In "Symmetrical Companion," the lovers "shall be two daring acrobats / above the staring faces / framed in wheels of light / visible to millions. . . . we shall not fall / as long as our gaze is not severed."

"Unloosed, unharnessed, turned back to the wild by love," Swenson writes in "The School of Desire." "Our discipline was mutual and the art / that spun our dual beauty. While you wheeled / in flawless stride apart / I, in glittering boots to the fulcrum heeled, / need hardly signal."

Other poems recreate centaurs in similar cadence, and one imagines Laocoön lovingly held fast by the serpent's coils. Titled "Laocoön Dream Recorded in Diary Dated 1943," the poet details the seven "arms" encircling her in erotic images: "an odd thrill made a geyser in my blood," she writes, after "an arm . . . / but longer than an arm . . . lapped me twice. / . . . One supple coil lay neat about my waist / . . . the other . . . slipped / to my hip. . . . This love had a new taste."

But setting these role-playing poems aside, the majority of Swenson's love poems are human you-and-I poems, or we poems, exquisitely tender and understated, as in "Holding the Towel," when the poet, on shore, begins to panic: "My squint / lost you to nibbling / waves." When her lover surfaces, her relief is enormous, but all she permits herself is: "I was still / scanning the nearby / nowhere-going boats."

In "In the Yard," the freight of the poem is pulled by the quirky, apt, almost brusque imagery of birds Swenson observes as she awaits her lover's return. The woodpecker, "Redheaded's riddling the phone pole"; the oriole, "cheddar under black bold head"; the pheasant, "the ringneck who / noseblows twice parades his mate." And then, casually, "You're back barefoot brought some fruit. / Split me an apple. We'll get red // white halves each our / juice on the Indian spread." As is often true in poetry, less is more. Much is withheld for the good of the poem.

And what a sure voice Swenson has, whether with the looks and sounds of birds or with bees, as in "A Couple": "A bee / rolls / in the yellow / rose. Does she / invite his hairy / rub? // He scrubs / himself / in her creamy / folds; / a bullet, soft, imposes / her spiral and, spinning, burrows / to her dewy / shadows." Equally deft, an artlessly simple yet equally erotic poem about a dandelion, "Little lion face / . . . streaked flanges of your silk / sunwheel relaxed in wide / dilation," broadens to these images: "You're / twisted shut as a burr, / neck drooped unconscious, // an inert, limp bundle, / a furled cocoon . . . Oh, lift your young neck, / open and expand to your // lover, hot light."

These truncated quotations cannot begin to reproduce the music Swenson creates with the resources of prosody. She is inventive but always linguistically accurate: "Shall we live like the lizard / in the frost of denial?" she asks alliteratively. Elsewhere, she employs assonance, "I gloated on the palomino of your flanks"; and personification, "hidden in the hair / the spiral Ear / waits to

Suck sound // and sly beneath its / ledge the Eye to Spear / the fish of light."

In 1970 May Swenson published a collection of so-called concrete poems, poems placed on the page to form shapes, that she titled *Iconographs*. She seemed to hunger for a new symbiosis that went beyond the format of line and stanza and she found it in these experimental, idiosyncratic structures. It was her ambition, she explains in a note to that book, "to cause an instant eye-to-eye encounter with each poem even before it is read word-after-word."

Two of her most successful concrete poems, "Bleeding" and "A Trellis for R.," are included in this collection. The first of these is often reprinted because of its inviting shape. It is set typographically so that a jagged cut runs vertically down the page. The two speakers, knife and cut, parry back and forth in a perplexing dialogue that ends: "I feel I have to bleed to feel I think said the cut. / I don't I don't have to feel said the knife drying now becoming shiny." Is the poet's intent philosophical rather than sexual? Perhaps. Or is this an emotional, even sado-masochistic, dialogue between lovers?

"A Trellis for R.," daring in its time, is Swenson's most overtly sexual poem. It is driven by the design of a lattice for roses she has established on the page, one which would be difficult to reproduce in this text. But consider these images: "Pink lips the serrate / folds taste smooth / and rosehip round the center / bud I suck. I milknip / your two blue / skeined blown rose / beauties too to sniff their / berries' blood up stiff pink tips."

Lesbian poetry is now so much a part of our culture as to be taken for granted. Excepting the poem just cited, think of the lengths Swenson went to to preserve her secret "love that does not dare to say its name" from a hostile world. And even after its social acceptance, Swenson, like her friend Elizabeth Bishop, maintained her distance from woman-identified poetry.

Still, poems encrypted for safety's sake, such as "Poet to Tiger," come down to us now with a resilience and charm they might not otherwise have had. "Come breathe on me rough pard / put soft paws here," the poet entreats. "Tiger don't scold me / don't make me comb my hair outdoors. // Cuff me careful. Lick don't / crunch. Make last what's yours."

Perhaps without knowing, in "Found in Diary Dated May 29, 1973," Swenson sums up for us the power and pleasure of her work: "Most of what is happening is hidden. / There is a subworld / Where the roots of things exist."

III. COUNTRY LIVING

GEESE-GO-SOUTH MOON

Early in October, in Geese-Go-South Moon, leaves rain down with a muffled sideslipping sound. Dust motes spin in sunlight like flour sifting in puffs onto the beginnings of batter. For the horses this season is heavenly. We haven't had a killing frost yet. All of our fields are open to them, and they wander like sleepwalkers from one area to another, grazing intermittently, sometimes standing for long thoughtful moments silhouetted against the backdrop of forest or granite outcropping.

This is the season when tails at last become superfluous. The biting insects have fled. Except for small ectoplasms of gnats that still hover in the quiet air, all is benign and salving in the ether. Gone the vicious little trapezoidal deerflies that draw blood from animal and human. Vanished too the bot- and horseflies. The ubiquitous blackflies, that penance of the North Country, never quite disappear, but they are greatly diminished. And this summer's long tenure of mosquitoes appears to be over.

We are in the briefest and most beautiful moment of stasis. Along the perimeter of the pastures, fall-flowering asters, tiny blue florets with yellow centers, flourish. A few late blackberries go on ripening, pursued by the greedy broodmare, who rolls back her lips in order to nip them off, one or two at a time, without getting pricked by the thorns. Jerusalem artichokes, harbingers of frost, are in bud and threaten to open in today's sunlight. Toads have begun retreating to the woods after a long and profitable summer, deprived of their prey now in the vegetable garden.

It was a good autumn for apples everywhere. We bought a bushel of drops from the local orchard and put up several quarts of applesauce, to say nothing of an assortment of heirloom species to eat out of hand. The gnarled and often wormy ones from our own trees get fed to the horses for nightly treats. Apple cider—what would autumn be without sweet apple cider?—comes from the same orchard and will be on sale for a few more weeks. I am told by reliable sources that old-timers store a gallon or two of cider in the back of the barn and let it ferment and freeze. By January what hasn't frozen is a powerful potion known as apple-jack, a homemade brandy.

Our wild pear tree, pruned as far up as man on ladder with loppers could reach, bore respectably this year. Hours of human labor, painless when spent in tandem with the Red Sox baseball game on television, peeled and quartered these nameless fruits and preserved them in pint jars fortified with strips of candied ginger. There aren't enough pears even to contemplate trying to make pearjack; just as well.

Mushrooms appear everywhere—two brain puffballs in the dressage ring, little pear-shaped lycoperdons dotting the pine duff like misplaced miniature golf balls, smoky hygrophorus clustering in the dark corners of the pine grove. Ripe honey mushrooms bloom at the bases of decaying oaks, the white talc of their spores dusting onto the mushrooms lower down in the garland and sprinkling the earth below these as if from a can of baby powder. Sometimes, traversing the woods on horseback, we spot a full shelf of oyster mushrooms swelling on the trunk of a dying tree. Reaping where you did not sow is a happy concept but it usually entails more work than is worthwhile. Some mush-rooms dry well enough, especially if started with a session in the microwave, then finished in warm sunlight. The plentiful honey mushrooms are easy enough to pick over, slice, and sauté in olive oil (or butter). Then they can be frozen for reuse in practically everything: spaghetti sauce, casseroles, or soups. Oyster mushrooms combine deliciously with scrambled eggs, but they are good enough to stand on their own.

The dogs are eager to accompany us in the woods, now that the languorous days of summer are over. The long-haired part-shepherd leaps into every muddy wallow; the all-white part-spitz digs energetically at a crevice between tree roots where he smells chipmunk, then bursts ahead of us down the trail, the flag of his tail waving joyously. Whether on horseback or on foot, this is the season to explore our second-growth forest.

Every day is more precious than the preceding. Daylight diminishes as the foliage flames with color. Dusk comes earlier in sharper air. We are approaching the end of a season you could follow as gleaners once followed the harvest, up from the Mid-Atlantic states, up through Pennsylvania and the Great Lakes, on to the Adirondacks and into New England. It still surprises me to see along the edges of hayfields those enormous round bales put by for cattle, resembling nothing quite so much as pillows for giants in an ancient fairy tale, a sort of reverse anachronism. More and more often I come upon these immense rollers already tucked into pillowcases of white plastic. The traveling eye encounters them as mysterious giants lurking at the forest boundary.

Mown fields represent the happy results of the harvest just past, the wheat grain gathered and stored, the timothy and clover grasses compressed, sometimes along with alfalfa, either into square bales to be stacked in dry barns for horses and sheep or rolled, as above. Keats called this a "season of mists and mellow fruitfulness" in his famous poem, "Ode to Autumn," the poem he wrote during a pastoral interlude in early nineteenth-century Winchester, a cathedral town southwest of London where autumn lingered a little longer. It's not often that we encounter in correspondence the exact instant of the poet's inspiration. In a letter to his benefactor Richard Woodhouse, Keats confided in artless iambics, "I never lik'd these stubbled fields so much as now—Aye better than the chilly green of spring. Somehow a stubble plain looks warm—in the same way that some pictures look warm—this struck me so much in my Sunday's walk that I composed upon it."

Today, like Keats, I am looking at autumn from the far edge of summer, and a somewhat elegiac note creeps in. The season of jam- and jelly-making is over. Gone are the cucumbers that I transmogrified into bread-and-butter pickles, the excess zucchinis that were grated and baked into squash bread, then frozen for cold winter nights. Peas, beans, corn repose in plastic bags in the freezer. Potatoes and onions are drying on screens on the glassed-in front porch. The vegetable garden is a lonely, tattered place; only the flags of leeks still wave there, along with a few remaining trees of brussels sprouts. Everything proclaims: we are reluctant. We are ready. But unlike Keats, whose last autumn that was—the following September he was off to Italy and an untimely death—I look ahead with the imperfect confidence age confers to another "season of mists and mellow fruitfulness."

BREEDING HORSES

The tenth baby in our amateur career of raising horses is "in the oven" here on our hillside farm in central New Hampshire. Three foals ago we dubbed a newborn "Final Filly," but we don't seem able to stop. I, at least, am unwilling to give up this grand annual gratification. The man I've been married to for forty-five years says *he* is ready to call it quits. But I note that unasked he's in the barn remounting the intercom attached to a ledge above the broodmare's stall. He's tuning in, readying himself for the impending arrival.

In a way unmatched by any other daydream, the prospect of another innocent on spindly legs racing across the pasture in midsummer takes the bite out of a New England winter. When I close my eyes on the night of a February blizzard I need to see healthy horses on broad pastures in my mind's eye, and among them an expectant mare or two. Victor, my husband and ally in this ongoing folly, is more detached. He will recount the nights of lost or fitful sleep, the suspense, the breeding fees, the angst of autumn weanings. A Johnny-come-lately where horses are concerned, he only took up riding, showing, and breeding fifteen years ago.

I, on the other hand, was born with my obsession. From kindergarten on I lobbied mightily for a pony. Before Christmas, before every birthday, I prayed ostentatiously on my knees under the bewildered gaze of my parents that a pony be granted me.

Failing a pony of my own, I took on the world's sad horses. I passed out my brothers' camp blankets to the occasional dobbin who still plodded by in our suburban neighborhood, hauling a cart full of garbage or clothes props. On a regular basis I filched sugar lumps from the kitchen pantry to have at the ready for any policeman's horse I chanced to encounter.

The most that was allotted me was an hour a week on the local livery stable's rental horses, faithful schoolies of no hope and little spirit who carried wistful children like me on their bony backs. I arrived early, stayed late, and appeared on nonriding days to make myself useful. Here I learned how to clean stalls, soap saddles and bridles, pick pebbles and manure out of elderly hooves. It was a useful beginning.

I never outgrew that childhood obsession, nor the impulse to rescue needy quadrupeds from bad situations. Luckily, in 1963, we came upon a derelict 200-odd-acre farm in New Hampshire in the heart of horse country. It was our plan to use it as a weekend retreat, a place for a family with three children (one of them a horse-crazy preadolescent female, a mirror image of her mother) to spend holidays.

Little by little as we began to reclaim the property, we also upgraded our equestrian skills. Even before we moved to the farm year-round, we took riding lessons, we boarded just-weaned foals over the summer, we rented trail horses for the same period and learned how to care for them. The eleven-year-old got her pony, an Arab-Welsh gelding, and was able to join Pony Club, her lifelong dream. He boarded just across town when his owner was absent.

In 1975, in full residence at last, we acquired an abused mare who had been slated for the slaughterhouse; indeed, we bought her from an intermediary by the pound. Of uncertain parentage but clearly part Standardbred, she and I bonded to the best of her ability—she had suffered too much to ever trust humans totally. Because she was given to wild bursts of runaway speed in the presence of other horses, we bred her to a local little Arabian stallion.

It was thought that motherhood would cure her of fleeing her wolves.

Our first foal was born in June 1976 in one of two box stalls we had constructed at ground level under the huge old dairy barn that came with the farm. Although the foaling was swift and easy, the mare rejected her offspring. Kicking and biting, she threatened to kill her. After a nightmarish twenty-four hours of restraining the mare and forcing her to submit to the foal's vigorous suckling so that the filly would obtain the vital antibody-rich colostrum, we separated them.

That baby grew up on a bottle. A cocky and opinionated youngster, she thrived on Borden's Foal-Lac and soon took her place in our small herd of horses. (As we added stalls, horses arrived to fill them.) At the age of four, our firstborn began feistily competing in twenty-five- and thirty-mile one-day competitive trail rides. Ultimately, she moved on to thirty-five-, fifty-, and hundred-mile trail rides in locations that ranged from Vermont to Maryland.

Arabians as a breed seem particularly suited to distance riding. They are slim and fleet, tireless at the trot, quick to size up the terrain and handle themselves accordingly. They form an abiding bond with their rider and they love to go forward. Aficionados of the breed often refer to them as "the dogs of the horse world" for their native intelligence.

In ten years not only had our orphan logged 2,000 miles in judged races but she had won several best-of-breed awards as a registered half-Arabian. Now a grave and bossy leader of the herd, dam of a stunning two-year-old, she is once again ponderously in foal. While she no longer competes, she is a pleasure horse and gets ridden almost daily. Finally, at the age of fifteen, she *is* a pleasure, unruffled by trailer trucks, wild turkeys, or flapping laundry.

As an integral part of the breeding process, I have logged a lot of white nights sleeping on the sawdust pile in a straight stall that abuts our biggest box stall. I move out to the barn when it appears to me that the mare is close to term. Her udder is full and hard, the muscles around her tail have softened. The bulge in her undercarriage that for months has looked like a fireplace log wedged sideways now appears to be moving backward. I begin to feel nervous about not being at her side all night long. Misgivings about what I hear over the intercom, rustlings and chuffings that I can't easily interpret, begin to overtake me.

This ordeal may extend from a few nights to two weeks. I try to soften it by hanging up a reading light in the stall. I refine my sleeping arrangements with two white pillowcased pillows, in spite of the sawdust that sifts into them nightly, and take along a thermos of something comforting to drink. Hot cocoa with a dash of coffee liqueur goes down well in a damp sleeping bag. Moreover, I try not to review in the dark all the breeding information, complete with horror stories, that I have amassed from attending clinics conducted by veterinarians or from the considerable literature on the subject.

Filtering out everything but happy outcomes is necessary to my well-being. At the same time, I move down to the barn prepared. On the shelf in the grain room I have assembled a package of sterile, elbow-length plastic gloves next to a tube of lubricant in the unlikely event that an emergency forces me to intervene. A bottle of iodine with a squirter attachment is ready to sterilize the umbilicus; preventing infection from entering through the newborn's navel is an important early step. There's a stack of worn bath towels for drying the baby, a pail and sponge for cleaning up the mother, a Fleet enema for the foal if it does not pass meconium soon after birth. The vet's phone number is engraved on my brainpan.

The mare is wearing her old leather foaling halter. We never, ever leave any of our horses unattended when they have halters on. An unbreakable nylon halter is an accident waiting to happen. This worn leather headpiece is guaranteed to come apart if she catches it on some unlikely protuberance. She wears it full-time now, just in case she needs to be caught and restrained.

Sleeping with animals is an education of sorts. I have learned how to doze through a wide variety of snuffling and snoring sounds, arisings and lyings-down, and how to come abruptly awake at the final, unmistakable sounds of beginning labor. This is invariably a moment of high drama, as the panting mare begins to circle restlessly and finally flops down with a harsh grunt. I beep the intercom that connects to our bedroom. Victor can pull on a pair of jeans and make it to the barn in ninety seconds (I have timed him).

He's wonderful to have on hand because he is calm and sensible. I am invariably in a state of exalted terror, telling myself to go slowly, move at half-speed, stay alert and relaxed so as not to transfer any of my own tension to the mare. I am focused on all the things that can go wrong, and on the fact that even at full siren, it will take our vet thirty minutes to get to us in an emergency. If, heaven forfend, there is a malpresentation—breech, for example—we will have to get the mare on her feet and walk her to delay contractions until the vet arrives. And failing that, the plastic gloves.

Most foals are born at night; nature seems to have selected darkness as a safer time for the mare to lie down and deliver her offspring. Because we had one stillbirth along the way when a foal was born with no one in attendance, I am determined to be present just in case any intervention is needed. It was heartbreaking ten years ago to wait out an eleven-month-long gestation only to lose a big, beautiful filly who never drew breath.

That was the firstborn of a very gentle quarter horse mare we had bred to a handsome Thoroughbred stallion. Presumably, the caul over the foal's nostrils never ruptured and the bewildered mother didn't intervene. I thought afterward that I had heard a kick in the barn just before dawn but didn't rouse myself to investigate. Some things we never forgive ourselves, even though that mare went on to deliver two other half-Thoroughbred fillies and is still an exemplary mother.

Despite my vigils, I have missed two other births—one by mere minutes when I went back to the house to get a cup of coffee, the second by half an hour when the quarter horse mare casually decided to foal out in the pasture in midmorning.

On that occasion, I had gone back to bed in the house at dawn with a terrible stomachache. Victor had fed and turned the horses out at 7 a.m., but hadn't segregated the expectant mare. He dutifully went out to check on her every hour throughout the morning, as he thought she looked imminent—there is no other word to express that slack-muscled stance when the foal has begun to move backward toward the birth canal—but the mother-to-be was still cropping grass and acting insouciant.

Just before noon he burst into the house to tell me the news. I staggered out with him to our farthest pasture to find a sturdy little filly up and nursing while my gelding was attempting to lick her dry.

A fine rain had just begun to fall. We had to make multiple trips to remove the terribly curious nonparents from the vicinity, and then we haltered the mare to begin the quarter-mile trek across the pasture and down a craggy hillside to the barn. The baby bopped along merrily, unfazed by the rain, terrain or distance. (She is now a big, bold jumper of four-foot fences.)

Obviously, we are amateur breeders. *Amateur* in the true sense of that word, "lover"; financially, it is a losing proposition. My other life, as a poet and writer, supports the horse passion. Here on Pobiz Farm the two of us supply most of the labor involved, but we must buy hay and grain, pay the farrier who trims and shoes our horses on a regular basis, and keep abreast of our vet bills. Routine health matters such as wormings and inoculations are within our expertise, but in any given year we are sure to encounter at least one ailment we are uncertain about treating on our own—an abscessed hoof, persistent cough, swollen knee, or exotic rash. When it comes to clearing more second-growth woodland to make pasture, digging postholes for our fences, repairing run-in sheds in the pastures and the like, we hire outside help and work along with them.

As amateur breeders and trainers, we raise youngsters to live out-of-doors as much as possible. They are invited into their stalls twice a day at feeding time and they are handled daily, groomed, fussed over, and taught from an early age the etiquette of behavior with humans. Unlike many show horses who are rarely out of the artificial environment of the barn or indoor arena, ours go out on the trail to encounter brooks and boulders and on the road to come to terms with trucks and bicycles and children. By the time they leave us they are road-wise and confident, though shaggier than their show-ring counterparts. Clearly, we do not operate at a profit.

Is it feasible to make money breeding in our corner of the world? A few stalwarts manage to hang on, usually through a combination of skills—boarding horses, training youngsters, showing horses for wealthy owners, teaching riding at levels ranging from rank beginner through fourth level dressage, as well as working with horses and riders in cross-country and stadium jumping. Breeding is better adapted to a warmer climate, where horses can be out on pasture most, if not quite all, of the year; where hay crops can run up to four or five cuttings in a season instead of the stingy two we can expect here in Zone Four. New Hampshire forage pastures, no matter how well-kept, cannot compete with Kentucky bluegrass. There, the limestone underlay makes for rich growth. Granite outcroppings, alas, do little to improve our timothy and clover.

A few outstanding stallions can be moneymakers for their owners in any geography. Winning racehorses retired to stud command huge breeding fees. Imported warmbloods—big Trakehners, Hanoverians, Oldenburgs, and the like—are very much in vogue right now. Televised show events have created a new interest in jumping competitions as well as in dressage, where horse and rider execute predetermined figures, comparable in some measure to those demanded in ice-skating competitions.

The big warmblooded horses, developed from skillful cross-breeding of Thoroughbreds and old-timey workhorses (some Arabian and Morgan loyalists have been known to refer to them as the warm dumbbloods) have for the most part wonderfully serene dispositions. While they may be bold movers with giant strides between fences, they are also remarkably tolerant of the tight discipline required in the dressage ring as well. A professional breeding establishment with one or two well-known stallions from Holland or Germany can indeed turn a profit from stud fees.

But Arabians never go out of style. There is always a demand for versatility and the Arabian can perform well in a variety of disciplines. In addition to marathoning and racing on the flat, this breed makes a refined carriage horse, a fancy saddle-seat show horse, an amiable Western pleasure mount, a talented dressage horse, a rewarding family pet. By and large, Arabians are not gifted jumpers because of their naturally elevated head-set, but there have been some notable exceptions.

Because of our interest in distance riding, we have gravitated toward crossbreeding with Standardbreds, the trotters of harness-racing fame. A bigger-boned, less refined, and generally more phlegmatic breed, the Standardbred can bring size and a slightly calmer attitude to the offspring. In my experience, the pure Arabian is not enormously tolerant of human foibles. Adding in the cooler blood of another breed, be it Appaloosa or quarter horse, Morgan or Standardbred, can ease the situation.

The rewards of breeding successive generations are largely aesthetic and personal. I can see my old runaway mare shining through her granddaughter, this three-quarter-Arabian filly who stands at the gate nickering for attention. She recognizes the car that has just driven up the hill; it may disgorge a person who will come down and speak to her. If, on the other hand, it's the monthly meter reader, she will ignore its passage.

I can also see, objectively, that this youngster is quite an improvement on her ancestor. Because we crossed a long-backed mare with an Arabian stallion, we developed a more closely coupled animal (the Arabian traditionally has one less vertebra than other breeds). She has her grandparent's broad chest and substantial heart girth, plenty of room for lungs to expand. While her graceful head with its dished profile and tiny ears are typically Arabian, her legs are not quite so fine as a pure Arabian's. She has good "bone" and solid joints. Her pasterns, the joints that connect the prominent bone of the lower leg to the foot itself, slope slightly more than is common in the Arabian. This gift came from her Standardbred ancestry, as did her powerful hindquarters and solid, round hooves. Here she carries a stronger musculature than the traditional Arabian, for if the Arabian has any consistent conformational defect, it can be seen in the sickle shape of the hind legs, the lighter bone, the deerlike oval hooves. This time we were lucky. The next cross may emphasize other, less sought-after traits: big Standardbred jughead and east-west-pointing ears, a short neck set low in the chest, a long back, a deep body on delicate legs.

Since we've only had two colts in ten rounds, chances are the unborn foal is a colt. Chances are it's a buckskin, or almost. The old hybrid mare was a liver chestnut; her descendants have dorsal stripes and bicolored manes and tails. The two-year-old is a buckskin. Her mother is a mouse dun. Another buckskin of the same size and conformation would be lovely—a potential driving pair.

On the other hand, at least we know it isn't twins. Our vet checked the mare with his ultrasound scanner when she was a mere three weeks along. The embryo then was little more than a dot on the screen. Ultrasound has become a major diagnostic tool in breeding. If multiple fetuses are detected, a skillful vet can pinch off all but one. For despite her size and strength, the mare cannot normally house two embryos. And almost always the mare will abort well before term. If she carries twins to term, rarely will both be born alive.

Final filly? Final colt? We couldn't be more ready.

FOREWORD TO *SAY THIS OF HORSES*

This well-researched and commodious anthology opens with a reproduction of Guillaume Apollinaire's charming horse calligram and proceeds from bits of the *Rigveda* to an excerpt from Chaucer's *The Knight's Tale*. It includes poets as disparate as Henry Wadsworth Longfellow and Lawrence Ferlinghetti and treats the reader to Dorothy Wellesley's little known but lively rhymed history of the horse, as well as Walt Whitman's "Stallion," May Swenson's "Bronco Busting, Event #1," James Wright's "A Blessing," Louise Bogan's "The Dream," and other familiar poems.

I am flattered to be represented in this ambitious compendium of horse poems that ranges so widely every taste will be gratified. Indeed, I can imagine readers poring over the table of contents in search of, say, Wallace Stevens's aristocratic "Polo Ponies Practicing"; Faye Kicknosway's moving narration of the lame old ploughhorse and the exhausted dirt farmer, "The Horse"; Donald Hall's justly famous "Names of Horses"; or Jane Hirshfield's "The Love of Aged Horses."

Yes, the horse has been a symbol of power and flight down the ages. The horse has been our enduring myth, the repository for our love and terror. The horse has been cruelly used and tenderly worshipped—and never, to my knowledge, have poems celebrating its existence been anthologized as extensively and with the degree of intellectual probity and earthy passion that *Say This of Horses* exhibits.

BEAUTIFUL SOUP

Even though winter has begun its slow downward slide, the dark still comes on far too early. By 4:30 the horses have lined up at the paddock fence to await their minimal rations of grain, followed by fat fluffed-out piles of hay. The dogs, as I said in an old poem, "grovel their desire / to go indoors, lie by the fire," and we two humans begin to think about the soups waiting in the basement freezer. "Soup of the evening, beautiful soup," the mock-turtle sang in *Alice in Wonderland,* "beautiful soup, so rich and green, waiting in a hot tureen." When winds howl and temperatures plummet, the prospect of hot soup and toasted cornbread for supper is positively tantalizing. Essentially, we have four choices: leek and potato soup, carrot and tarragon soup, butternut squash and pear soup, and broccoli-spinach soup. (There are also pints of pickled beets than can be magicked into soup in the blender, with the addition of yogurt. But this combination is best served cold and lies in limbo till the first hot days of June.)

This year, absent a killing frost till mid-November, we didn't pull our leeks until Halloween. Our potatoes, exhumed a few weeks earlier, lay on old screens on the front porch. Our onions had already been pulled, dried, braided onto baling twine, and hung decoratively from a harness hook in the kitchen. All of these freezer soups begin in the same way and take happily to one's own addenda or omissions. We cut open, rinse assiduously to remove any remaining flecks of grit, then chop into bite-size pieces our fattest leeks, and braise them with at least one big chopped onion in olive oil (butter of course is better) until all are golden and softening. Over these, we pour enough packaged broth, either chicken or vegetable, to drown the addition of a couple of peeled, chopped potatoes. (Needless to say, homemade broth would be better.) We then add a little salt and some honest pepper, and simmer till potatoes are soft. Finally, we buzz this concoction in the blender, thinning with extra broth to attain desired viscosity. This is delicious as is, but you have the option of adding some cream (in our case, fat-free half-and-half).

Carrot soup is much the same, except for the addition of a handful of tarragon leaves, carefully plucked from their stalks. Here too a very late frost meant we still had lots of live tarragon flattened up against the house foundation on the south side, but the dried variety works equally well. Butternut squash is peeled, cut into small squares, steamed in broth; peeled and quartered pears are added when the vegetable begins to soften, some dollops of grated ginger may be added, and the concoction goes into the blender. And the broccoli-spinach soup is a way to use up the little florets that persist in forming even after the first frosts, together with whatever scissors' snippets of spinach can be obtained from the long row that follows the pea fence. I'm not above sprinkling in a handful of arugula, if it's still viable. How precious these last live things from the garden seem! To this soup we have usually added minced garlic from the grocery store, but this fall I finally planted about forty slivers of a pink Italian cultivar cadged from a wise organic gardener. I took the time to mark where they are hibernating in the kitchen garden, as volunteers of romaine, cilantro, parsley, and red mustard will spring up in this same patch next April. I mean to be garlic-independent by this time next year.

If you haven't put up any soups of your own, if you're thumbing through dried mixes in the supermarket or opening cans as winter turns the corner, maybe this article is something to clip and file. Or maybe you'll just be inspired by the memory of it next fall to experiment on your own. Cauliflower soup, for instance. Fresh pea soup, with mint. "Soup of the evening, beautiful soup."

SPINACH

Is there anyone out there who remembers the cartoon character Popeye the Sailor Man? "I fights to the finish / 'cause I eats my spinach," he preached to millions of twentieth-century American children staring at small portions of the green stuff on their supper plates.

A member of the goosefoot family, spinach comes in a variety of leaf forms, from deeply savoyed—crumply—to almost perfectly smooth. The former has aesthetic appeal, the latter, ease of cleaning. All varieties, despite the claims of January's illustrated seed catalogs, are subject to bolting, which means they go to seed in midsummer or hot weather. Some last longer than others, but practically everyone agrees that the best way to get a good spinach crop is to start seeds early—"as soon as the ground can be worked," goes the mantra—and then plan for another crop in the fall.

The problem is, by the first of August, when home gardeners like me should be on their knees preparing fresh plantings of spinach and kale, lettuce and new baby radishes, we are exhausted. I garden organically, without recourse to any sprays except for one made from the seeds of the venerable neem tree, which grows wild across much of Asia and Africa. This means, if pests arrive, I have to spray vigorously every other day, and even more attentively after a rain. The rest of our far-too-ambitious garden is peaking. The first blueberries and the last raspberries cry out to be harvested. The kitchen becomes a factory for blanching and freezing the overabundance of ripe vegetables, from beans to broccoli, and putting up jams and pickles.

Really, really fresh spinach, picked in the afternoon and eaten at the evening meal, is unsurpassable. Young leaves make a delectable salad. Cooked, it takes kindly to all sorts of sauces and potages. It freezes well, too, after quick blanching. But somehow there is never enough of it. Growing alongside it in the garden, however, is a weed that deserves a better fate than being yanked out and tossed on the compost heap.

Lamb's-quarter, *Chenopodium album,* is a wild spinach that can simply be added to the cultivated spinach leaves. (It also goes by various unappetizing folk-names: pigweed, goosefoot, muck-weed, dungweed.) Once I learned to recognize it as an edible invader in my garden, I found whole stands of it growing wild in the pastures (the horses will not touch it). I find it a great additive. To test its spinach-y flavor, I gathered a sizable batch in late spring, then cooked and froze it. When I thawed and prepared it in mid-February, no one could tell it from the cultivated product.

Three spinachlike alternatives are more readily available as packeted seeds. One is New Zealand spinach, *Tetragonia tetragonioides,* also called Botany Bay greens or New Zealand ice plant. According to a wonderful book, *Vegetables from Amaranth to Zucchini,* by Elizabeth Schneider (William Morrow, 2001), its cultivated seeds first showed up in the New World in records of the New York Horticultural Society in 1827. But my bible among seed catalogs, Pinetree Garden Seeds of Gloucester, Maine, claims that it "has been in use in this country since long before the Constitution. It is a staple of the dooryard gardens at Sturbridge Village."

Even so, New Zealand spinach has yet to take the American gardener by storm. One good reason to grow it is that it can be depended on to flourish all summer and that when treated like spinach, tastes very much like it, though somewhat milder. (Raw, it's a dud.) I add it with impunity to my picking basket. But just as often, I cook it independently. Like true spinach, tetragone, as Schneider calls it, takes kindly to chopping and blending with cream cheese, yogurt, sour cream, and other sauces.

Another spinach substitute, Malabar spinach, is touted in several standard catalogs. Widely cultivated in Malaysia and India, *Basella alba* serves as a foundation planting at the Epcot Center in Orlando. Its trellising habit is a useful quality in a small garden; it will climb whatever is provided. But, citing Schneider once again, "Basella is a love-it or leave-it vegetable, like okra—and for the same reason: sliminess."

To be honest, I tried it only one season. In its favor, it climbs; it is easy to trellis and thus saves space. But it *is* slimy and this characteristic caused everyone in the family to testify against it.

But a new cultivar, named Perpetual Spinach, has made its way into my garden, thanks to seeds from a local gardener. It does not bolt, it puts up huge leaves on sturdy stalks, and it lasts, well, not forever, but almost. I finally found it in the Thompson and Morgan catalog, which admits it is actually a member of the beet family. Nevertheless, they list it on their spinach page and I have found it a very welcome addition to the garden. Planted early in spring, it survives all summer and grows merrily into late fall, and I suspect if I mulched it heavily it would make it through the winter. In every way it behaves like spinach, though the taste is somewhat stronger. I sauté onion and garlic in my big nonstick frying pan, then add shredded Perpetuals and braise with a bit of broth to the desired doneness.

A last nod to Popeye. Like him, "I eats my spinach."

The Wings of Winter

I never heard a gull laugh until my husband and I went to
Rockport, Texas. A little Gulf Coast town full of bait shops
and boats for hire and decrepit piers where great blue herons
somnolently perch, waiting for their perfect fish to swim by, it
was a casual paradise for us New Englanders. We were stunned
by the scene. Our birding skills were limited to chickadees and
nuthatches, tufted titmice and purple finches, hardy types that
spend the winters with us in New Hampshire.

At home, our most spectacular bird is the pileated woodpecker couple that drops in from time to time to pluck the
bittersweet that is slowly strangling one of our enormous ash
trees. We put out suet for the downy and hairy woodpeckers
and we startle every time a horde of evening grosbeaks swoops in
with their yellow and black scapulars to clean out the feeder in
minutes.

Seven years ago, we bought two used-up gravel pits that
abutted our property. With the help of a small grant and a lot
of sweat equity we gradually restored them as wildlife preserves.
Now more wild turkeys than porcupines bed down there (and we
much prefer them). Grouse and partridge scoot airborne when
we walk through to see how the crab-apple saplings are faring.
But with a barn full of horses needing looking after, we could be,
we thought, only casual watchers of the winged.

We had come to Rockport just for a long weekend—to thaw out, relax, admire a 360-degree horizon. Curiosity almost instantly pricked us into action. With a decent pair of binoculars and the guidance of local friends, we went from spectacle to spectacle: sandhill cranes bobbing around the dry reeds of their favorite habitat; roseate spoonbills feeding—or, more accurately, shoveling—in the marshes; the long-billed curlew, whose incurving beak is a miracle of engineering; quick-stepping willets and greater yellowlegs; coots and scoters, skimmers, mergansers, pelicans; and our own common loon, down from Maine to disport in these warm waters. We saw almost a hundred species of birds the first day.

On the second day, we climbed aboard Cap'n Ted's *Whooping Crane* for a trip up the coastline of the Aransas National Wildlife Refuge and saw 22 of the 317 whoopers known to live in the wild. Just to catch a glimpse of the snow-white five-foot-tall whooping cranes is an epiphany. They are still gravely endangered. They mate for life and make the perilous journey north via the Platte River in Nebraska all the way to Canada for nesting season and back. And because they don't begin to breed until they are three years old, raising this tiny remnant to a stable population will take years of vigilance.

Two days was hardly enough. A month at leisure would have been better, but we squeezed out a third day to take the free ferry across the Corpus Christi ship channel to Mustang Island. Bottlenose dolphins played alongside the boat and brown pelicans dove for fish in our wake. Along the approaching shore, we saw black skimmers and oystercatchers.

At Port Aransas's Tarpon Inn, where FDR once was celebrated for the giant tarpon he hauled from those waters, we came upon the Port Aransas Birding Center. On the elevated boardwalk that extends into the freshwater marsh, we accepted several offers to peer through serious birders' scopes at cinnamon teals, black-bellied whistling ducks, black-necked stilts, and lots more roseate spoonbills.

So many earnest humans paying obeisance to the birds! Such respectful observation, such camaraderie among the binoculared, monoculared, tripodded, and unencumbered gives this participant hope. Every acre we set aside represents us at our best.

Back once again in New Hampshire, we took to wearing binocs around our necks whenever we crisscrossed the old gravel pits reborn as wildlife management areas. With our renewed stealth, that spring we regularly spotted birds we might have missed before: a busy kestrel working the peak of the rise; a scarlet tanager; and briefly, almost unbelievably, a pair of indigo buntings. Late one afternoon we flushed a string of turkeys and two ruffed grouse. No great rarities in these woods, but while we enjoyed them through our lenses, a large grayish blur intervened. Refocusing, we melted behind some scrub and waited deferentially as a cow moose meandered by, down the incline that had so recently been a raw gravel-cut, to the stream below, like the manifestation of a larger idea.

HIGH GROUND

There is no perennial virgin like an inveterate gardener in February. Year after year, we foresee glories of the earth to come: luxuriant blooms, groaning harvests. Who among us in February remembers the brilliant mistakes of the past?

Take last year. The entire onion crop in my thirty-by-thirty-foot home garden failed. Most years I get enough mature globes to braid with baling twine and hang in the kitchen for bragging rights. Whenever I need an onion, which is often, I just lop off the bottommost one (and sweep up the chaff of dried skins that fall to the floor). But last year's summer was persistently dry. It followed an unusually wet spring. Possibly there were sunspots or planetary misalignments to blame as well. More likely, I set them out too soon, before the slender stalks sprouted from seeds I started indoors had been hardened off properly.

Most respectable home farmers buy onion sets that need only to be stuffed into place once the ground unfreezes. But special onions—my beloved Ailsa Craigs, for instance—aren't to be found in sets. Most people are content with hothouse veggie plants of tomatoes and peppers, broccoli and cabbage. But not me. Who wants to forgo the challenge of raising your own from seed? It's like achieving handsome, charming, well-mannered children and sending them off to an Ivy League school—all in one season. Admittedly, there are some failures.

Growing useful organic vegetables is certainly one part narcissism. (The remaining two parts are gluttony and pride.) But since my garden is environmentally sound, my pride is at least somewhat mitigated by civic responsibility. And then there's the soul-crying need to outface winter just as the solstice turns. The days are getting longer, yes, but—an old New England saying—"when the days begin to lengthen / then the cold begins to strengthen." This year, I promised myself, I would get a decent head start. And I did, patiently twitching seeds into place during a raging nor'easter.

Now it is March and our house is full of makeshift shelves supporting miscroscopic greenery thrusting toward fluorescent lights, like a vegetative neonatal ward. But this year it's not just edibles. "You have to watch out for these perennial campanulas," the local nurseryman told me when I windowshopped along his hothouse rows last fall. "They take over your whole garden."

That was just what I longed for. A carpet of bellflowers surrounding our dying willow tree! Blue bellflowers running riot down the slope, pouring across into the sheep pasture! But the campanula seeds I sent for last December—seeds that proved so tiny they asked to be planted one by one at the end of a moistened toothpick—are now only half an inch high. At least I have learned new respect for the horticulturists who raise perennials professionally, cosseting them to maturity by the million.

To everything its season. The hardy onions, broccoli, cauliflower, brussels sprouts, and cabbages that are currently crowding us out of the house will emigrate to the glassed-in, south-facing porch as soon as the nights stay above freezing. In mid-April they'll go into the garden, long before it's time to even think about starting corn.

Corn! Homegrown corn! The crop that exacts the most labor and on an annual yield basis gives the least. But—pride, gluttony—it's worth it.

Presprouting seeds on the cozy sunporch thwarts the crows who otherwise will steal every single one as soon as it's planted. Last year, on a distinctly chilly May 15—outside temperature forty-eight degrees—I inserted eighty-four seeds into potting soil and covered the cells with plastic. Over the next seven to ten days, seventy-eight seedlings emerged, poking out of their kernels like half-fledged chicks. I kept them moist. I turned the trays around daily, to take advantage of their heliotropic nature. I prayed over them a lot, too, hoping to coax some sign of life from the six duds, but to no avail.

By the sixth of June, the stalwarts were four to six inches tall. Cautiously popping them out of their containers, cupping their stringy roots like strands of pearls, I set them out in the garden.

We ate our first ears on August 9; they were ambrosial. But who knows what this year will bring? Bellflowers, perhaps.

Bear

This year on our horse farm in central New Hampshire, we are visited regularly by an enormous black bear who comes at dusk and makes himself at home under the bird feeder. The feeder is suspended from a pole, a good six feet above the ground. This bear is so tall that he simply sits on his haunches, one knee cocked, wraps his forelegs around the cylinder, and patiently sucks sunflower seeds out of the apertures with his tongue. After a while, the cocked knee appears to develop a cramp; he languidly stretches it out in front of him and cocks the other leg. This performance is wonderful to watch but we try to remember to take the feeder in at sunset so as not to contribute to the delinquency of the species.

Everybody in the family has crept out onto the deck to snap pictures of "our bear" in the gloaming. But the blueberry farm just above us has more than birdseed to worry about. It is likely the same bear marauding their pick-your-own bushes. Not content with stealing blueberries, he rolls around in the plantings, creating havoc. The owners have tried wrapping bacon strips around the electric fences. They theorize that the thief will be attracted to the bacon, sniff it, and receive a shock to his only penetrable part.

Occasionally, out horseback riding, we've met a black bear or two. We've waited respectfully for a cub, sunning himself in the middle of the trail, to depart. Once a bear loped alongside us down the bridle path, unnervingly close, finally swerving off into the woods.

To my surprise, our horses were less afraid of these ursine encounters than of meeting pigs. A favorite route took us past one of those old-fashioned family farms where pigs rooted freely with noisy abandon in a large pasture. The horses hated this scene. They snorted and plunged and begged to turn back until we urged them to gallop past.

Late one afternoon last summer I walked uphill to my vegetable patch above the house to pick green beans for supper. A bear was sitting under the teepee of saplings that housed my Kentucky Wonders. A swarm of mosquitoes haloed him as he gorged on clusters of beans. Not until he had dispensed with the entire crop did he rise and amble off into the woods. "Beans and more beans," I said in a poem, "for this hour of bear."

Last spring, on my way to the barn at daybreak, I saw—and heard—our dog nose to nose with a female bear who was outgrowling him. Her two cubs, meanwhile, had shot up a skinny pine tree to which they clung like shipwrecked mariners. Once the dog was retrieved (See how obedient I am? he seemed to say to her. When they call me, I come!), we watched entranced as she exerted all her maternal skills, including pretending to leave them forever, to coax her youngsters down.

I don't want to succumb to rural rapture and brag about "our" bears. I know we are seeing them more frequently because humans are encroaching on their habitat. But living in precarious harmony with *Ursus americanus* feeds me as fully as our home-grown vegetables do.

How We Found Our Dog

When we lost a much-loved little Mexican street dog last fall we began to search the various adoption sites for an adult dog to keep Virgil, our ten-year-old hound dog, company. Preferably a mutt: we're convinced they're smarter than purebreds. Not too heavy to lift into the sink for baths: we have a horse farm and all our dogs have found horse manure irresistible—to eat and to roll in. Finding a small grown-up dog in New England wasn't as easy as it sounds. There were plenty of Lab and rottie and shepherd mixes but few lightweights available.

Finally, we found and adopted, after extensive paper and phone interviews, a little brown dog from Tennessee. Ten-year-old Rosie came in a trailer truckload of at least a hundred dogs shipped up from the South to a park-and-ride beside the highway about fifty miles south of our farm in New Hampshire. Terrified at first, she gradually absorbed the house, barn, and acreage as her very own dynasty. She didn't know much but proved a fast learner. A week to become house-trained. Six more to master walking on a loop leash and simple commands: Come, Sit, Stay, Off! (She is a tireless jumper-up on people and big dogs and, alas, can't always resist.)

Watching Rosie adapt to her new freedom has been enormously rewarding. Apparently, she had been found in a house with several dogs and a corpse, dead five days. She has a deep scar on one shoulder from the dogfights that finally alerted neighbors to call the police. Rescued, she spent her outside hours secured to an overhead run and nights indoors confined to a crate. Other dogs in her foster home were adopted; she remained. Perhaps her looks were not appealing enough. Yes, she's somewhat strangely proportioned but her appearance grows on you. What breed is she? One part bat (the ears), one part anteater (the nose), the rest some sort of terrier. She runs like a deer, stalks frogs like a heron, and rolls wriggling on the grass like a puppy.

Once we were satisfied that she would not run off, we allowed her to accompany us off-leash to the pond, the pastures, the barn. She trolls the horses' stalls for any tidbit of dropped grain, spends hours paddling around the perimeter of the pond, fascinated by the small plops of water striders, the occasional emergence of a turtle. She walks on stone walls, loves to ride in the golf cart to the vegetable garden, and indoors migrates from chair to chair to couch—but not to beds, forbidden.

When we took Rosie to the vet for vaccination against Lyme disease, serious in New England but not a problem in the South, we learned that she has a severe heart murmur. Now she gets a daily pill wrapped in something yummy. And of course Virgil also gets something yummy, without a pill. He's very tolerant of his new companion. In her exuberance she frequently jumps on him and he never protests. Although he has slowed down from his earlier turbulent years of racing in woods and fields, baying as he went, Rosie inspires him to run to keep up with her. She is our sixth rescue in a line of superior remarkable special outstanding mongrels. Our vet, who has looked after every one of them, tells us that Rosie, despite her ticker, despite her just-visible cataracts, could live another ten years. But even if she has only this one in paradise, it will be a memorable one.

SETTLED IN AT HOME

"How the same old pump of joy restarts for me, going home!" I wrote years ago in a poem, and it is still true. Flying back on that late March day from giving a reading or teaching a class, I was overcome with longing to return to familiar surroundings: the old farmhouse, the dogs, barn cats, horses, as well as the human family. The landscape I had left was fulsome with forsythia, dogwood, daffodils, and tulips. The landscape I returned to was dingy and brown, laced with remnants of snow. It was, nevertheless, home.

Home has acquired a sharper meaning. More than ever, home has become our refuge, our sanity; our intimate connections are centered there. Home steadies us with its certainty, with the humble routines of dailiness, its chores and grocery lists, its welcome drawing down of blinds at the end of the day.

For many years, I lived in the suburbs, with husband, three children, dog, a lawn, petunias, and one maple tree. Our house, a modest Cape Cod Colonial, was carpeted. It had a dining room, silver tableware, crystal, good china. In 1963, when the children were still young, we bought an abandoned farm in New Hampshire, thinking to use it as a weekend getaway and summer retreat. For years, we camped out in it like gypsies. Provisioning was haphazard; we never knew how many adolescents would be spending the night on the living-room floor. Saturday and Sunday mornings, after feeding them, they could be motivated to cut brush along the path to the pond, heft stones back into place on the ancient walls, or shovel snow from the overloaded porch roof.

No substantial renovation took place until we moved in year-round. Then we embarked on a new roof, the first of numberless capital expenses. There were sills to replace, and several rotted clapboards. One woodstove had a crack in it. You could see daylight through the back when you bent down to stuff newspaper and kindling in, so it was replaced with a modern, airtight model. After ten years, in the middle of the coldest winter of them all, we broke down and installed a propane heater down cellar that warms the first floor, at least.

The house, built in 1800 and eternally in need of repairs, still sits at the top of a hill on a dead-end dirt road. What we love most about it is the fact that it is half a mile from anywhere. In winter when the leaves are down, we grudgingly suffer a distant hum from the highway. Above us, owners of a pick-your-own blueberry farm sometimes snowshoe down for a visit. Below us, the kind of good neighbor with many trucks who pulls you out of a snowbank you've skidded into.

The restored pastures are miniature alps giving way to granite outcroppings and dense woods. We became adept at digging post-holes and constructing three-board fences that zigzag in our best approximation of a straight line to enclose the first two fields. Beyond these, we set up electric fences along the perimeter of fields abutting the forest but over the years we've allowed them to stand unelectrified. Swinging the hammer, I became ambidextrous as we built one run-in shed ourselves. Victor worked with a hired hand to build the other two sheds.

We saved half of the tumbledown three-story barn. Built into the hill, it once sheltered dairy cows on the first floor, with a convenient opening to the manure pit below. We found a mason who shored up half the foundation that encircled the manure pit but wouldn't touch the other half, a mass of boulders that looked as though someone had exploded the original wall. Four years later we found a mason willing to undertake removal of that tumble of stones. Victor designed and together we roughed in six stalls, plus a narrow space for grain, and a water box that fortuitously feeds a steady flow from the barn's artesian well, another capital expense. In addition to housing the horses the barn provides enormous storage space for, among other items, old storm windows, an early dishwasher, seven abandoned toasters, heirloom skis and snowshoes, a Ping-Pong table, and a staggering array of tools.

Thirty-seven years of hard labor have brought us to this comfortable and comforting place. The grown children and their families return to it periodically, with palpable nostalgia. *Remember the toboggan slide we built, all the way from the upper pond down around Devil's Elbow? Remember the Scrabble games on the floor of the Cozy Room* (their name for the birthing parlor)*? The throw-the-Frisbee-across-the-pond contests? The butternut-tree swing, the logs we split, the wood we stacked, the day the grape jelly boiled over? Remember when both mares had their foals on the same night?*

An eat-in kitchen with a commodious table has replaced the suburban dining room. When everyone assembles at the same time, we are happily hard-pressed to find enough chairs. Broadloom has given way to bright area rugs, crystal and china to baskets and wooden bowls. My study upstairs overlooks the barn and paddock on one side and, on the other, part of the broodmare pasture. Even though, as a bewildered visitor put it, we "really do live in the woods," even though nights are so quiet I can hear a horse cough and a distant owl hoot, "who cooks for you-u-u?," I am in touch with the outside world. I am online, possess a fax, a copier, an answering machine, and an elderly IBM Selectric for addressing envelopes and clattering out ideas for poems.

I cherish my solitude, but it has its imperfections. The proud old farmhouse, barn-red with white trim, gladdens my heart every time I come up the hill. But the wide-board pine floors require upkeep. The exposed chestnut beams collect massive cobwebs. Field mice come indoors after the first hard frost and scamper overhead all winter. Feeding two woodstoves means tracking in bits of leaves and tattered bark. Sometimes the recalcitrant water pump requires thumping by an experienced hand. All too frequently, we endure electrical outages. And while the town plows us out after every snowfall, we are usually last on the list.

In the early years, my suburban garden consisted of a few haphazard perennials left by the previous owner, supplemented with store-bought packs of petunias. I remember setting out a handful of tomato plants that sulked in the dappled shade cast by our one tree. House plants bored me. Many a philodendron died of neglect in my indifferent care.

My transformation into an enthusiastic organic vegetable gardener was gradual. Soon after we moved full-time to the farm, I discovered the joys of reading colorful seed catalogs in January, especially during a howling blizzard. I closed my eyes and fantasized about sturdy wire-mesh fencing, raised beds, rotted horse manure magicking into humus, intensive planting. Next, I began starting some seedlings indoors, under the fluorescent lights that frame the kitchen window. Infinitesimal seeds emerged from potting soil and put up true leaves, then branched into recognizable lettuce plants.

Meanwhile, there was a late-spring or early-summer foal to anticipate every year. A pregnant mare to cherish with extra vitamins and daily attention to the thickness of the bedding in her stall. Nothing shortens winter like expectation, both animal and vegetable. In a sense that Rilke never intended, I "await[ed] the birth-hour of a new clarity."

Although our house is not prepossessing enough to be featured in the town history, I think with awe and respect of the lives, both animal and human, that unfolded here. In the front hall hangs a broken marble gravestone that commemorates the death of five-month-old Walter Colby in January 1826. I think of the attic beams, enormous chestnut-tree trunks that must have been winched into place by oxen and manpower. I think of the stillborn foal we buried behind the barn in a hymn of early June mosquitoes. Of six dogs, who spent long lives of uncomplicated freedom here.

Mostly, I think how deeply rooted I am in this place. And how I expect to stay here to the end.